DITCH YO

FIND YOU

NO • EGO

"Telling, transparent, and transformational.
A handbook for dreamers, visionaries,
and all who desire the best out of their life.
–Bishop Jamie Englehart
President of C.I.M. Author, Speaker, Overseer – Bay City, MI

FOREWORD BY ASHLEY TERRADEZ

PHILLIP MCKINNEY

No Ego

Copyright © 2019 Phil McKinney

Published by Kherington House
www.kheringtonhouse.com

Scripture quotations marked TPT are from The Passion Translation®. Copyright © 2017, 2018 by Passion & Fire Ministries, Inc. Used by permission. All rights reserved. ThePassionTranslation.com.

ISBN: 978-1-943157-82-2
Printed in the United States of America

For more information or to contact the author:
www.noegocc.com

Dedication

I dedicate this book to my wife, Becky. You have always made me want to live up to the man that you see in me.

And to our children Grace, Isiac, Isiah, and Gideon. I have learned more from you than you have learned from me. The blessing of God on my life is revealed in you. I love you.

Foreword

This is the book you never knew you needed!

None of us would want to admit we have an ego. We're smart enough to know that being egotistical is not a virtue and definitely not a reputation we want to have.

On the contrary, the ego can be the biggest hindrance in our lives, preventing us from success and fulfilled happiness. It can hinder our professional careers, our emotions, and sabotage our most important relationships. We all need to know how to address this monster in our lives. We need an "anti-ego coach!"

In this humorous, inspiring, and often challenging book, Pastor Phil gives easily applicable, practical wisdom on how to ditch your ego and become all that God made you to be! Phil dares to be so open and honest, and at times dangerously vulnerable – a refreshing change from most other leadership or motivational books. Phil's wisdom and down-to-earth writing will empower and equip you to reach your full potential in life.

I have the honor of knowing Phil personally, having spent time with his family and his staff, so I have seen him live every sentence of this book first-hand! He has used his personal experiences, decades of study and mentorships, along with timeless wisdom from the Scriptures to create a powerful resource for anyone wanting to ditch their ego.

If you know that your ego can often get out of control, and even cause you problems, this book is for you. If you don't think you have any issues with ego, then this book is definitely for you! I dare you to read this book and apply the principles to your life today!

The only thing you have to lose is your ego.

– Ashley Terradez is an international speaker, author, and Bible school instructor. After graduating Charis Bible College and being ordained by Andrew Wommack, Ashley and his wife, Carlie, founded Terradez Ministries. Terradez Ministries is a teaching and miracle ministry with offices, distribution centers, and prayer phone lines in North America, Europe, and Africa. Ashley is a sought-after church and conference speaker and his television program, Abundant Life, reaches 250 million households daily on terrestrial, cable, and satellite networks. For over 20 years, Ashley has been dedicated to empowering believers in the promises of God all over the world!

Contents

Introduction

As children we never needed permission to dream, imagine, or play make believe. We created realities in our imaginations and stories of what we would do when we grew up. Places we would visit, people we would meet, and lives we would save.

At an early age we were celebrated for our creative, limitless thinking, and told that we could do whatever we put our minds to. But then something happened – we grew up. The voices that once encouraged dreaming, imagining, and limitless possibilities are traded for words like reasonable, responsible, and practical.

We are led to believe that maturity is staying in our lane, not creating waves, and following social norms. As a result, many of us are living a life of routine that feels like a requirement, instead of living a life of adventure that feels like a reward.

I have always wanted to make a difference. To lead a life of significance and leave a legacy that my children would be proud of. Heroic, right? On paper for sure, but internally I questioned if it was for the right reasons. I had to stand toe to toe with my motives and ask the difficult question, *"Am I doing this to make a difference or to make a name for myself?"*

There is a distinct difference between the reward of being used to make a difference and the need to be applauded. It is one thing to be caught doing a good deed but quite another to go out of your way to make sure people know what you did. It is self-centered, self-absorbed, and arrogant. It's ego. What I recently discovered is that ego has another characteristic that is much easier to miss and justify.

On an ordinary November day, in the center of a crowded parking lot, I had one of the most impactful moments of my life. I had dropped two of my sons off at an indoor trampoline park and had an hour and a half to myself. I decided that instead of driving all the way back home only to return, I would just enjoy the quiet time in my car. I always have a book with me, so I parked my car in the middle of the lot and began reading.

I don't know if it was the noise of someone getting in their car that caused me to look up or if I was just pausing between chapters, but I began to look around at all the cars around me. There must have been a couple of hundred cars in the parking lot that day. Vehicles owned by people that I may never meet, know, or ever even hear of. I thought to myself, *"Am I just another person in the sea of humanity that may or may not have a significant impact on the world?"*

The moment evolved and quickly became precious – reverent even. I wasn't just surrounded by cars anymore, I was surrounded by people. I was overcome with compassion and an awareness of how important they were to God. I was looking at cars, but I was praying for people. At one point I said, *"Lord, I want to do more. I want to make a bigger difference. I want to have a greater influence."*

And in the stillness of the moment, my eyes streaming with tears, I heard a whisper from within me say, *"You can, just ditch your ego."*

To say that I was shocked is an understatement. In my estimation, my prayer was heroic and others-focused. *"How is that egotistical?"* I thought.

The best way I can describe what happened next is to say that it was more of an awareness than a voice. Doesn't make sense. To be sure, it was a divine download that was about to transform my life.

I was keenly aware of how ego had been dominating me and keeping me from pursuing my God-given dreams because I was filled with insecurity, fear. I was also occupied with people's opinions. It is no less egotistical to be consumed with self-doubt, to be fearful of leaving others behind, and to be obsessed with people's opinions, than to believe you are the greatest of all time. "You" are still at the center of it all, and if you want to change the world, you're going to have to ditch your ego, too. It is not a one-time decision that makes everything become magically better. It's a lifelong commitment to a process of becoming more, not just doing more. It's an *"inside"* job that will require you to face difficult realities about yourself, but the reward far outweighs discomfort.

The purpose of *NO EGO* is to speak to the dreamer and to resurrect the creative, limitless possibilities within you. There is nothing reasonable about a God-sized dream, and He would never give you a dream that could be fulfilled without Him. Your future is not ahead of you, it's within you. You are uniquely gifted and impregnated with greatness. It is God's plan for you to be wildly successful, because your success is for the benefit of us all. Ditch your ego and find your dream.

> *"I am the sprouting vine and you're my branches. As you live in union with me as your source, fruitfulness will stream from within you – but when you live separated from me you are powerless. If a person is separated from me, he is discarded; such branches are gathered up and thrown into the fire to be burned. But if you live in life-union with me and if my words live powerfully within you – then you can ask whatever you desire, and it will be done. When your lives bear abundant fruit, you demonstrate that you are my mature disciples who glorify my Father!"* – Jesus (John 15:5-8 TPT)

CHAPTER 1

Moving Forward

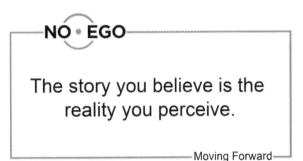

"*I am prepared to go anywhere, provided it be forward.*" – David Livingstone

Master Mechanic

Have you ever noticed how easy it is to diagnosis and "*fix*" someone else's life? I am masterful at fixing your problems! Mine, not so much.

It seems perfectly clear to me as I meet with people that if they would make this change, add that process, and stop doing that thing, they'd be golden. And by the way, why didn't they see it themselves?

Perspective

I like to run people through this simple exercise to illustrate how this happens. Bring your hand up in front of your face, palm facing you, nearly touching your nose. Looking through your fingers, find something to focus on in the room. The illusion makes your hand appear larger than the object you are staring at. As you slowly pull your hand away from your face, you realize that your hand is much smaller than the object.

Circumstances have a way of getting in your face and would have us believing that they are bigger than they are. It takes another person with a different perspective to help us see what is really going on.

Chaos Is Loud

Life also has a way of turning up the volume on us. It's like traveling to a place that you've never been and the stereo in the car is blaring. Your spouse is sitting in the passenger seat trying to tell you directions, and you don't hear a word they're saying. They are frustrated because you're not responding, and you are getting angry because they are not helping you. "Can't they see that I'm struggling over here?"

What is really going on? We need to turn down the volume.

It's Never One at a Time

What about all these decisions we need to make? Deadlines we need to meet? Promises we need to keep? Goals we wrote down in January ... maybe we'll start on Monday.

Before we know it, we are in survival mode. So, what do we tend to do? We toss the decision into the ever-mounting pile in the future and postpone progress. Before long, the pile is so tall and overwhelming, the hope of getting ahead seems lost.

Who Has Time for Dreaming?

"Dreams?" we say under our breath with barely enough restraint to keep our eyes from rolling when someone asks.

What is your go-to response? Perhaps you've used some of mine? Responses like,

"It's been busy…"

"When things slow down…"

"When the economy turns around…"

"When we get this paid off…"

Who Are We Kidding?

The only thing worse than those responses is that we believe them. Ouch. That sentence stings. You might be thinking, "Now just hold it right there. Things have been busy!"

That may be true, but when is the last time they weren't? When is the last time things slowed down? Even if they did, life has a way of introducing new demands. With every season of life, we have new and mounting expectations that all fight for our time. The effect the economy has on us is far more to do with us than we like to admit. The economy has transitional times, ebbs and flows, and seasons of plenty and seasons of drought.

This is not a unique or new challenge for the free market. In fact, some of the world's biggest and most successful companies were started during a recessionary period such as Hyatt, Lexis Nexis, Fed Ex, Microsoft, CNN, GE, HP, and many others. The founders for those companies recognized a need and were able to fill the need successfully.

In order to move forward we're going to have to address the anchor that is holding us from moving forward – ego.

Ego?

That's right, ego. Perhaps the reason we miss this is because we limit the meaning of egotistical to the self-absorbed, conversation hijacker who somehow turns the focus of every story back on themselves. The guy who always one-ups your story and is continuously looking for their reflection in anything that will give them one more glimpse of their greatness. We all know and loathe these people in our lives.

But why do they bother us so much? Easy, because they are so self-centered! And it's true they are but so is the person who continues to put off their dreams.

It's just a little easier to justify because we camouflage it in "humility." We'll come back to that later.

Let's Get Real

Webster-Merriam Dictionary defines ego as "One of the three divisions of the psyche in psychoanalytic theory that serves as the organized conscious mediator between the person and reality. Functioning both in the perception of and adaptation of reality."

In other words, the lens by which we see the world is the world that we perceive in our minds. Even if it's not reality.

I Can't Believe My Eyes!

I grew up on a small farm in rural Michigan. Less than ten miles from our house was a small country General Store. This store had a small kitchen in the back that served square pizza. As far as I knew, this was the only place on the planet that had square pizza.

On certain occasions, usually on a Friday night, we could talk my mom into ordering pizza from the General Store. This old building had a hand-painted advertisement sign on the broadside of the building. It was strategically placed on the exterior wall facing the pothole-infested dirt parking lot. The paint was faded and cracking but still readable. The painted sign listed the variety of items that the store carried on its shelves.

Warning! *(The story gets a little vulgar.)*

My step-brother had been telling me that the old painted sign on the side of the General Store ended with the phrase *"Everything from soup to your nuts."*

My semi-innocent eight-year-old mind was on tilt. "No way!" I exclaimed.

There was no way that this type of vulgarity would be allowed in our small farm community. The time had finally come to call his bluff. We rode along with my mom to pick up our square pizza from the General Store.

When we arrived, we parked squarely in front of the sign in question. I couldn't wait to read it out loud and see it for myself. My mother hopped out of the car and made her way into the store while I feverishly read the sign.

As I got to the final line and read aloud *"…everything from soup to your nuts,"* I gasped. No way! I could not believe it. My step-brother was right. But how?

Just then my mother returned to the car. Before she was even capable of handing the pizza off, I was already pointing, shouting, and trying to get her to read the sign, too. I felt like I was getting away with something by simply reading such a thing. How was I to get in trouble if it was in plain sight for everyone to read?

My poor mother was trying to wrap her head around what had happened to wind me up in the short time she had been inside.

"Read it! Read it!" I kept repeating while pointing at the sign in front of our windshield.

As she read it out loud, I was inching up on the edge of the seat just waiting for the words to come out of her mouth. Line after line I was losing patience. *"Just skip ahead and read the last five words already!"* I thought in my head.

Then it happened *"…everything from soup to your nuts"* I heard her read out loud.

"See!" I shouted as I watched her lips form the final syllables. *"How can they get away with that?"* I demanded to know.

"Get away with what?" she retorted with a puzzled and half amused smirk.

"That last line!" I shot back with amazement at a whole new level.

My own mother didn't recoil at what she had just read out loud to her eight-year-old son? She slowly turned her focus back on the sign, leading with her eyes first, and then slowly turning her head. Straight to the last line and like before, reading out loud but very slowly this time "...everything...from...soup...to...nuts."

My eyes getting slightly wider with each word as my neck protruded, head turning to stick my ear toward her in order to hear her better.

Wait, what? What did she say? My head whipped back to the sign as I read it again silently in my head.

Only this time the word "your" was not there. It never was. It had always said *"Everything from soup to nuts."*

What Happened?

I had been told a story by my step-brother. And, at a subconscious level, I believed it. It was like I was programmed. Even though the word was not on that old painted sign, I saw it. I imposed it. It became my reality.

I have discovered that this phenomenon happens in other areas of my life. In all areas of my life. Remember the definition of "ego" I shared earlier where ego acts as "a mediator between the person and reality especially by functioning both in the perception of and adaptation of reality."

The story I believe is the reality that I perceive.

What's Your Story?

What have you been programmed to believe that is altering your perception of reality? Moving forward requires action to be sure, but what actions you take or if you take any at all, must first begin with what you believe.

What you believe shows up in your reactions. Especially under stress. An old friend of mine, a pastor, tells a great story to illustrate this point. One Sunday he was assisting his church in connecting the dots on this point.

The story as he tells it goes like this:

> Imagine right in the middle of the Sunday morning service the church phone rings on the other end of the line is the United States Air Force. The officer begins with a short apology and gets straight to the point. *"Moments ago, during a routine test flight, one of our fighter pilots mistakenly released a bomb, and in less than three minutes the bomb is going to hit your church. You need to evacuate the building immediately."*
>
> The administrative assistant burst into the auditorium, disrupting the pastor's message, and begins to relay this shocking news. *"We have less than three minutes to evacuate the building before the bomb destroys it and kills us."*

What's the Point?

If you believed the report to be true, you would immediately evacuate the premises. If you rejected the announcement in disbelief, you would stay put and likely mock all the frantic parishioners as they ran for the door.

Either way, what you believe dictates your actions.

The quality of your life is in large part a reflection of what you believe about yourself. It is my invitation at the onset of this book to "ditch your ego."

Unloading your ego is like untying the rope from the dock and setting sail on a great new adventure. Leaving the shoreline of familiarity is scary, but no one discovers new worlds by clinging to what they already know. The journey will include rough waters, opposing winds, and some violent storms.

All of which are designed to help you, not destroy you. The excursion is filled with unknowns, but with the right crew, equipment, and tools, you'll have what it takes to navigate through it all.

What If?

There is great power in your "What if?" The words that follow your "What if?" will either keep you fastened to the life that you know or will empower you to pursue your dreams.

What if I'm right?

Let's go!

CHAPTER 2

Know It All

NO • EGO

All of heaven is available to those who are poor enough to receive it.

——— Humility ———

"One cannot learn what they think they already know." – Epictetus

"There Was This Time in '84..."

Actually, it was closer to '81, but once you tell a story, you are kind of stuck with the details you first used. Anyway, the one-liner is the start of a sarcastic response I gave to one of my sons for being wrong about something that I was sure I was right about.

The implication was that I am wrong so infrequently that it hadn't happened since 1984.

The story goes like this:

I was about four years old and had entered a heated argument with my grandmother about what the phrase "PJs" stood for. You see, I had it in my head that my new Incredible Hulk sneakers were not in fact called "sneakers" but called "PJs."

She was adamant that my PJs were what I slept in, not what you wear on your feet.

"What is wrong with you?" I thought. *"Why are we even having this discussion?"* I was right. I knew it. *"Why is she laughing at my frustration?"*

I had reached the limit of my tolerance with Grandma and decided to wait until Grandpa got home. He was my biggest fan. My most powerful ally.

I don't need to tell you what happened; you already know that sneakers go on your feet and PJs are what you sleep in. Grandpa was awesome. He let me down gently with Grandma perched in the background with that *"I told you so" raised eyebrow expression.*

So now it's a running joke between my son and me. Whenever it appears that I may be wrong about something, we say in harmony, "There was this time in '84."

Things You Know That Just Aren't So

Nearly forty years later, I would love to say that I had learned my lesson in Grandmother's kitchen, but life has provided me plenty of opportunities to demonstrate that I can be a slow learner.

There is a coin company near where I live whose owner does a weekly radio spot called *"Things you know that just aren't so."* The radio spots are a few minutes long, and he dives into interesting facts about commonly accepted topics that turn out not to be true.

I have even found myself staying in my car a few extra minutes after arriving at my destination to finish listening to his ads. The stories always seem to have a bit of "shock factor" when he reveals the misconception, wives' tale, or distortion of fact.

For me, it only primes the pump to ask more questions. *"What other things do I 'know' that just aren't so?"*

Why?

Over the past ten years I have been on a journey of furious curiosity. I have always been a curious individual even to my detriment. My mother tells a story of a time when I was a toddler. I simultaneously asked, *"Is this hot?"* while reaching out and touching the glowing red burner at the same time.

Over the past decade, this journey has led me to question everything I believe. It has been transformational, liberating, and empowering. It is something that I have gotten better at over time, too.

When I first began, it was in response to beliefs and ideas that felt conditional, hypocritical, or disempowering. It has gotten much deeper in recent years, as I began to question things that seemingly don't need to be questioned. Topics, ideas, and fundamental beliefs that seemed to be established as standard knowledge.

When you start questioning, you learn to ask better questions.

I cannot understate the impact this has had on me. It began subtly but has grown into this unquenchable hunger to question everything. Not in a hostile argumentative way. In most cases, quite the opposite. Perhaps Stephen Covey says it better than anyone: *"Seek first to understand before being understood."*

In Covey's book *Seven Habits of Highly Effective People*, he shares a wealth of knowledge and wisdom, but it was those seven words that hit me at a soul level. It revealed my need to be right. To know the answer. To know it all. It bruised my ego if didn't.

My ego had to go!

You Talk Too Much

I am a communicator. I express myself with words. I noticed an ugly thing about myself as I began a new journey of "Seeking first to understand before being understood." I learned that in areas that I was most insecure about, I talked the most.

What was I doing? I was attempting to prove to my listener or audience that I really knew it all.

I was also trying to prove to myself that I knew more than I really did.

I See You!

Author and speaker Patrick Lencioni has a saying that opened my eyes. He simply states, *"If you spot it, you've got it."*

In other words, the very thing that you notice in others, you know the thing that grates on your nerves, it's usually a good indicator that you have the same issue. Go ahead and let that sink in for minute.

You, like me, are probably going back in your memory and having to choose whether you want to be honest with yourself. You don't want it to be true. It stings. I know.

If we connect Covey's statement, "*Seeking first to understand before being understood,*" with Lencionni's observation, "*If you spot it, you've got,*" it helps us to identify patterns and behaviors. For example, when I am in a conversation with someone or sitting in an audience and a person is speaking on a topic that they clearly don't know enough about, evidenced by the fact that they are running on and on, I know why.

Whereas I would normally get annoyed, I can employ Lencionni's observation of "If you spot it, you've got it" and marry it to Covey's wisdom of "Seeking first to understand before being understood."

Instead of reacting or worse, over-reacting, I need to be humble. I need to ditch my ego and remember I too wrestle with the same condition, Know-it-all-itis. I know why they are acting like Know-it-alls! Because they don't know it all, and their ego won't let them be honest or open.

There is a great quote by Jesus captured by one of his inner circle guys named Matthew. It is a clip from one of Jesus's sermons. There are so many people interested in what Jesus had to say, that on this occasion, He had to position Himself on the side of a mountain in order for everyone to hear Him. Theologians and historians would later reference this event as His "Sermon on the Mount."

The profoundness of His words is frequently lost on modern day Christianity because we miss that He was changing the script of Jewish tradition, laws, and requirements. Most of our English translations subtitle the passage as the "Beatitudes." I want to draw your attention to the first of nine beatitudes. Jesus said, *"Blessed are the poor in spirit, for theirs is the kingdom of heaven."*

This bible verse messed with me for many years. I mean how are you "blessed" and "poor" at the same time? And how does this involve heaven?

My "Aha!" moment came a few years ago while listening to my friend Steve Eden. Steve is a pastor and a dynamic teacher. On one such occasion I had the good fortune of listening to him speak to a group of leaders. I am a note taker and was busy writing as fast as I could.

That is until he made this one statement. I stopped writing and let the words soak in like a marinade. He paraphrased the verse, and it came alive to me. Steve said to the audience, *"All of heaven is available to those who are poor enough to receive it."*

I whipped my head to look at the person next to me with a look that said, *"Did you catch that?"*

Jesus is telling His listening audience that there is no limit to what is available so long as you are not so rich on "self." This timeless truth carries the same weight two thousand years later.

There is no limit to what is available to you and me as long as we will ditch our ego.

So Where Do We begin?

I've heard it said, *"Every great journey begins with a single step."* This phrase is more valuable than just a catchy Hallmark card! When we look at the gap between where we are and where we want to go, it is easy to get discouraged. Discouraged before we even begin. And some don't begin.

You don't need faith to finish, you need faith to begin. It helps to encourage yourself by looking at other areas of your life where you're seeing good results. Let's go after making the "good" areas "great" in a minute, but first let's identify some areas that we're not getting the results we want or expect.

It is my guess that it isn't a matter of desire or attempts. You are likely putting in the work and doing everything you know to do. Depending on how long you have been at it, you may be at your wits end. Or just flat ticked off!

I've been there. It is usually at this stage that we begin to compare ourselves with others who are getting results in the area that you want to succeed in. Comparison is almost always rooted in hatred. Hatred of self or hatred of others.

If we haven't ditched our ego yet, the thoughts usually run along the lines of:

"It must be nice."

"I would be successful too if I had the same parents, opportunities, money, location, breaks, etc...."

"They must be doing something immoral, crooked, or cheating the system."

Maybe your thoughts aren't as "PG" as my examples, but nonetheless we have tendencies to start chopping them down like a tree.

And why do we do this? Because it feels better to believe that they are cheating the system than it is to believe they might know something we don't.

Keep Your Nose in Your Own Row

Another observation I have made is that we tend to compare and make our analysis of people we don't even know. We see them on T.V., YouTube, social media, and vlogs. We see their books, products, endorsements, and fame, but in most cases, we don't actually know them.

Yet we form an opinion based on some troll's commentary on Facebook or Instagram, and because it makes us feel better about the lack of progress on our dreams, we accept it as fact. We feel emboldened to share this juicy insider information on our social media feeds and in conversations with others as if we are in the know.

I've done it. My upper lip is curling in disgust with what I am capable of when my ego is in the driver's seat.

It's like we revert to a fourth-grade version of ourselves, secretly passing a note to a classmate that reveals that Tommy has "cooties." To make matters worse, there is no shortage of people who are willing to receive your note, agree with you, add to it, and pass it on.

If this analogy is insulting to you, that was the intent. Sometimes the truth must offend us before it can change us. I know it had to for me.

The tipping point for me was when I ran out of people and public figures to slander. I was standing alone in the carnage, and when I had no one else to find fault with, I had to face reality.

The problem was me, not them. I had to ditch my ego.

Birds of a Feather

I'm sure you have heard the old phrase "Birds of a feather, flock together." We have a habit of congregating with like-minded people. They become our tribe. Our people.

I knew I was missing something, and when I began to look around at my "tribe," I noticed we were all getting similar results. And they weren't good. *"There must be more!"* I thought.

I had concluded that I no longer wanted to do life this way, and so I began to spark conversations among other leaders in my circle. Instead of making accusations about people outside of our tribe, I began asking questions about our methods, our philosophies, and our beliefs. It wasn't well received.

What I know now, that I didn't know then, was that when you begin to question methods, philosophies, and beliefs, it threatens ego. And just like CBS's hit show *Survivor*, I was voted out of my tribe.

It was jarring, painful, and lonely. I became the target of ridicule and suspicion. I was reaping what I had sowed.

The most difficult and lengthy challenge for me was guarding my heart. I needed to have thick skin while not allowing my heart to become hardened or callused.

This is important, and you should take careful note of this point. Most of the things that were said about me were not accurate or true, and the primary reason that I wanted to defend myself was because it bruised my ego.

Though it didn't seem like it at the time, it turned out to be a gift. It helped me to ditch my ego.

CHAPTER 3

You Need Help!

---NO • EGO----------------

Accelerated growth is fueled by
helping others.

——————————————— Serve —

*"The only difference between criticism and feedback
is how you hear it."* – Tim Grover

Minor Adjustment, Big Gain

Have you ever been given advice so simple that it's
almost insulting? It usually comes after you're
exhausted and have tried *"everything"* (a word
exhausted people insert).

I don't know which is more infuriating, the fact that
you haven't actually tried *"everything"* or that the
suggestion is so elementary that it is an insult to your
intelligence.

Well, before you scrap the whole thing in a fury of frustration, consider the advice offered to me by a brilliant mentor that has saved me time, money, and energy. Four simple words: *"One-eighth inch adjustment."*

Billy Epperhart was a standout pitcher on his high school baseball team. Even though he was one of the best, he knew it was a long shot to play ball at the college level. His skill and determination earned an opportunity to play for Oral Roberts University as a starting pitcher. It was the season opener, and Billy was at the mound.

His debut was not the start he had hoped for. He wanted to prove to himself, his team, and his coach that he deserved to be there. With the bases loaded, he felt his college playing dreams and his scholarship slipping away. The movement near the bench caught the corner of Billy's eye. Looking toward the baseline, he noticed the coach calling timeout as he made his way to the pitching mound.

"This is it," Billy thought. *"I blew my chance and coach is going to pull me."*

After what seemed like an eternity, coach finally made it to the mound and calmly said, *"You seem to be having trouble with the slider."*

Billy nodded his head in agreement, but before he could respond, the coach began to speak again. *"Let me see how you're holding the ball, son,"* the coach requested.

Puzzled by the request, Billy thought, *"Am I pitching so poorly that he is questioning whether or not I know how to hold the ball?"*

Billy reached his hand into his glove to retrieve the ball and pulled it out with the ball firmly placed between his thumb, pointer, and middle finger. With his palm facing up, he revealed the ball and his finger placement to the coach.

Without a word, the coach reached down and adjusted the ball placement in Billy's hand by one-eighth inch of a turn. *"Give that a try,"* he said as he turned and walked back toward the bench.

And guess what? One batter after another, Billy was striking them all out. Instead of the coach pulling him from the game, he made one minor adjustment that made all the difference.

Too Deep, Too Fast

When the pressure is on, it is easy to go too deep too fast. As I mentioned in the previous chapter, I worked many years troubleshooting and repairing electro/mechanical issues in a variety of environments and manufacturing settings. One thing that manufacturing operations have in common is that they have little tolerance for equipment downtime. It doesn't matter if you are producing a widget for a car or a diagnostic test kit for the CDC, if production stops, pressure mounts.

Most manufacturing environments know how much money the company is losing each minute the machines are not producing. There are production goals for departments or divisions, and managers are held accountable for their output. The pressure to produce gets passed on to the operators, and they must give an account for their productivity.

Tradesmen are paid a generous wage for their experience and expertise but are expected to diagnose and make quality repairs quickly. Though I was far from the best in the industry, one thing that helped me a great deal was ruling out simple repairs before tearing a machine apart.

Years ago, I was working for a large office furniture manufacturer in Wisconsin and received a call from an upset machine operator. Betty was an angry woman in her mid-sixties and, simply put, was *"unpleasant"* to be around.

Remember *The Wizard of Oz?* In the beginning of the 1939 classic, the fictional character Almira Gulch is a bitter neighbor who wants to take away Dorothy's dog, Toto. The scene begins with Mrs. Gulch riding her bike with conspicuously eerie music playing in the background.

You may already know where I am going with this. Betty was a dead ringer for Mrs. Gulch. Not only did Betty look just like Mrs. Gulch, her attitude and tone of voice were perfect matches as well. When I heard her voice on the other end of the phone, I cringed and kicked myself for being the one who answered the call. *"This aluminum saw is still not fixed,"* she screamed into the phone. *"I told you guys about this yesterday, and you told me it would be repaired before morning,"* she continued.

I didn't wait for a pause, I just interjected, *"We're on our way, Betty!"* and hung up the phone.

The walk from one end of this massive facility to the other took a few minutes, and as I approached the department, I heard the bellowing voice of Betty long

33

before I saw her. It didn't make matters any better that I had hung the phone up on her in mid-rant.

She wasn't done giving me her piece of mind, and once she saw me coming, she didn't wait for me to get into range to start firing off profanities like a loaded cannon.

As I approached the saw, I ignored her. Well, I pretended that I was ignoring her. This only added fuel to her fire, and the attacks became personal. *"You over-paid, lazy, pathetic maintenance technicians couldn't fix a sandwich let alone a piece of machinery!"* she shouted at me.

It took less than ten seconds to discover the problem with Ms. Betty's saw. Without saying a word, I turned and looked at her until we locked eyes. I stared for a few seconds for dramatic effect, then I slowly turned my head while keeping my eyes locked on hers. Only at the final moment did I turn my eyes hoping that she would follow my gaze. I reached down, grabbed the cord, and plugged her saw into the outlet.

Without speaking (but sticking my tongue out in my imagination), I gave her a slight smirk, turned, and waved as I walked away.

The Pressure Is On!

We love it when the story ends with us riding off into the sunset as the credits roll, but let's be honest, there are times that we're just plain stuck. The bases are loaded, the machine is still broken, the business is at a standstill, the relationship is stalled, and the pressure is mounting.

Robert Horry says, *"Pressure can burst pipes, but it can also make diamonds."*

The choice is ours to make. It is like being stuck in mud or drowning in water. You can keep giving it more oomph, but you're not getting out of the situation without help. You need a tow or a rescue.

There is a choice to be made. Allow the pressure to crush you or form you into something valuable. Stay stuck or ditch your ego?

You may be thinking, *"I'm not stuck. I'm moving and performing every day."*

I think this is one of the most deceptive forms of being stuck. It's called a rut. Pastor Duane Sheriff once said, "The only difference between a rut and a grave is that a rut has the ends knocked out."

It's easy to mistake motion with momentum, activity with progress, or busyness for productivity. I have found that in most cases when you challenge a person's activity and busyness, they will defend it tooth and nail. Why? Because we place a higher value on intention than we do on accomplishment.

This mindset gets established in childhood when we give out participation trophies. We inadvertently groom our children to become fragile adults who are incapable of receiving instruction or constructive criticism. Even when the instruction would benefit their life.

Blind Spots

My family and I live in the beautiful State of Michigan. We have four distinct seasonal changes, but my absolute favorite is summer. I love the heat. Seriously, it cannot be too hot for me. I joke with my southern friends about this. I'll tell them, *"I was wired for the South, I'm just called to the North."*

The summer season is a short window for us in the north, and it takes until the middle of June before the Great Lakes reach a reasonable swimming temperature. At least in my opinion.

It has become my family's custom to get away and go on vacation the first week of July. It is hard to beat the beauty of Fourth of July fireworks over Lake Michigan.

The day had finally come, and my wife Becky and I were rushing around town to pick up some last-minute items before we took off for our much-anticipated vacation with the kids. We stopped at a small convenience store for a bag of ice. I didn't even bother to park in a proper parking space. I just whipped in the lot, parked parallel with the building, and jumped out. I dashed in and out of the store with nothing but sandy beaches, sunglasses, and sunburns on my mind.

In stride, I tossed the unopened bag of ice into the empty cooler in the back of the truck, jumped in the driver's seat, and reached for the shifter. *"We're off!"* I shouted to Becky, who was equally as eager to begin the vacation as I was.

I looked in the rearview mirror and waited a moment for the car behind me to pull out and make way. Like a dragster waiting for the light to turn green, I punched the gas pedal.

The sudden reverse action made Becky's body leave the seat and lean toward the dash. With equal force, she came slamming back against the seat as the truck came to a smashing halt. The force of her head slamming back into the seat was great enough to break her plastic hair clip in half.

"What in the world are you doing?" she yelled.

Honestly, I had no idea what had just happened. I knew I hit something, but what? I threw the truck back into park and jumped out to see what had happened.

The noise of the collision was loud enough that the store clerk heard it inside the building. He was walking outside to investigate while I made my way to the back of the truck.

I had run my truck squarely into a concrete-filled post. Painted brilliantly yellow I might add. The height of said post was below the bed of my truck, and when I looked out the rearview mirror, it was out of view. It was in my blind spot.

On the Lookout

We all have blind spots. We don't know that we have them because if we did, well, they wouldn't be blind spots anymore.

One detail that I left out about my collision with an immovable object was the fact that my truck is equipped with a reverse camera. Had I looked at the screen in my dash prior to reversing, I would have seen the pole in all its brilliant yellow glory. The camera was looking out for me and the screen was giving me feedback, but when you are in a rush to get to where you want to go, it is tempting to bypass the support that is available to you.

And like my poor truck did, you will come to a crashing stop, too. Ditch your ego. We all need help.

Exaggeration

Sometimes I exaggerate. Maybe you do, too. I love to fish. When I am telling a story about a great catch, it's easy to widen the gap between my hands a little further than I should when referencing the size of the fish. Or when re-telling a story, it can grow a little bit for dramatic effect to enhance the emotion of it all.

Don't leave me hanging out here as if you have no idea what I am talking about! Our minds also tend to exaggerate the length of time of our discomfort. This is how it happens for me, and perhaps you can relate.

There are seasons in life that are especially hectic. You know, early mornings, late nights, staff challenges, family struggles, budgetary concerns, or strained relationships. Sometimes all of this and more are happening at once.

It is during challenging seasons that our internal dialect can exaggerate the situation. We start using all-inclusive words like "always" and "never" when describing our lives. We exaggerate our internal story. Instead of recognizing that we are in a "season," we tell ourselves that this is how our life "always" is and that it will "never" change.

As Jim Rohn so cleverly illustrates, "For the past 5,000 years of recorded history, winter has always given way to spring."

We know something about long, harsh winters here in Michigan, and as long as some winters feel, Mr. Rohn is correct. Winter always gives way to spring. Neither seasons nor storms last forever.

Les Brown, one of the world's top motivational speakers, says it best, "*Storms do not come to stay. Storms come to pass!*"

Something's Got to Change

In 2010 I found myself being forcibly pushed around by the winds of change. It was a storm to be sure, but this storm didn't come to destroy me. It came to clear a path. I was in a strange dichotomy.

On one hand I felt illuminated, inspired, and hopeful that my dreams could come true. On the other hand, I was wounded, disappointed, guarded, and suspicious of anyone in leadership.

As I mentioned in the previous chapter, I had lost my people, my tribe. I was lost and searching for my identity, and one of the distinguishing characteristics of my previous tribe was fault-finding in others. Something that I shamefully participated in. I believe that we did this to rationalize our marginal success and impact. I had committed to stop doing this and start asking more questions.

I needed help! I didn't know where to begin, but one thing was undeniable. The people, groups, businesses, and ministries that I had previously been obsessed with cutting down were getting better results than I was. So, I started with all *"those people."*

I began to order book after book. I borrowed and purchased CDs and turned my car into a classroom. I was listening to TedTalks and watching YouTube videos. I positioned my laptop next to my bed at night and would fall asleep listening to sermons and messages. If someone mentioned a name or title that I had not heard before, I wrote it down and added it to my list. Nothing and nobody were off limits (except for clearly immoral things that violated my conscience).

What I was discovering blew me away. What I discovered was that nearly every person I previously deemed to be to be a liar, cheater, or heretic was a remarkable individual. Not only that, they also had a story of struggle that I knew nothing about.

Most of the time we discover or become aware of success stories because we can see the fruit of a successful person, enterprise, or ministry. What we conveniently neglect to do is research how they worked the soil, planted the seeds, tended the garden, withstood the seasons, and put in the time.

It was and is very humbling and humiliating to think back on all the effort I put into devaluing what took decades and even centuries to build.

Okay, I'll Come Already!

The real turning point for me came in February 2011. Some friends of mine who had made their "break" from the same group that I was affiliated with moved to Southeastern Oklahoma. They were some of my biggest cheerleaders and supporters.

They would call to check up on me and encourage me. We would share all the exciting new things we were learning. They too were involved in ministry and were now connected with another group. They went on and on about what they had found and how it was an entirely different culture than anything they had experienced.

I was happy for them, but I was gun shy and in no hurry to investigate. Finally, after what seemed like the one-hundredth invitation, they were adamant that I come and attend an upcoming pastors and leaders' conference their church was hosting. All I needed to do was fly down, and all other expenses would be covered.

What did I have to lose? It was February after all. It was substantially warmer in Southeastern Oklahoma than at home in wintery Michigan.

That's Different?

Full disclosure, I wasn't expecting much. When it came to church conferences I had "been there, done that." We arrived about thirty minutes early to get a parking spot and seat. The differences in what I had been accustomed to started right away, like in the parking lot.

The place was huge, and men were driving around in six-passenger golf carts providing rides from the parking lot to the entry door. "Okay, that's new for me," I thought.

But it wasn't the cart or the ride that stood out to me, it was the drivers. It is said that people make up their mind about a person, business, or church within the first seven seconds. These drivers were some of the nicest and most enthusiastic individuals that I had met in a while. And I was still in the parking lot.

Having spent years in the ministry at this point, I was acutely aware of all the activity that goes on behind the scenes to pull off a conference or special meeting. This was a large event with people coming from all over the country.

My friends spotted one of the Executive Leaders walking our way and grabbed him so that I could be introduced. I was delighted to be putting faces and names together and I was happy to shake his hand after my friend made the introduction.

Mr. Armstrong enthusiastically said, *"Phil, it's a pleasure to meet you! I have heard a lot of great things about you."*

Before I could finish my suspicion-filled thought, Mr. Armstrong continued. *"Would you like to grab a seat and get acquainted?"*

I am sure he noticed my furrowed eyebrows as I was trying to process the invitation, yet I was able to muster up a *"Sure? That would be great."*

So, we proceeded to a quiet space on the edge of the auditorium. You might be thinking, *"What's the big deal? The man only offered to get acquainted!"*

In my world, this was a paradigm shift. Senior and Executive level leaders didn't mingle with *"Average Joe"* attenders, and even if they wanted to, they had dozens of things going on behind the scenes that most know nothing about.

A "Game-Changer" Served Right Up!

I was looking for it. I was watching for signs. I was listening for innuendos because certainly there had to be a catch as to why this man would use the precious moments leading up to opening night to "get acquainted" with me. But there wasn't. No hint of façade, elitism, or jargon. Only genuine interest and appreciation for the fact that I had come nearly a thousand miles to attend.

The moment came when Mr. Armstrong did indeed need to attend to the conference, but before he walked away, he said something that I had never heard before. Words that would renew my hope in leaders and change the trajectory of my life. He looked me in the eyes and said, *"If there is anything that I can do to serve you while you are here, just let me know."* And with that he smiled, shook my hand, and walked away.

"Serve me?" I repeated in my head as I located my friends and found a seat.

"Well how did that go?" they asked anxiously.

Out of all the things we discussed, it was those two words that were repeating in my head that came out like an overflowing cup, *"Serve me?"* I am sure their facial expressions were only matching mine as they were trying to make sense of what I was saying. Was I repeating something I heard or making a request of them?

"Serve me?" my puzzled friends repeated.

"Yeah," I said with a breathy laugh as if to say, *"Can you believe it?"*

It took me a few minutes to add context to the statement for my friends, and it has taken me nine years to understand the implication of those words. Five words that rescued me, *"If I can serve you."*

Serving Your Way to Influence

The greatest Leader of all time changed the world, not by military force or domination, but by serving. The Gospel of Matthew records the words of Jesus, "For even the Son of Man did not come expecting to be served by everyone, but to serve everyone, and to give his life in exchange for the salvation of many."

Jesus is also recorded saying that the highest form of love among friends is to "lay one's life down for them." King Solomon, who is accredited as being the wisest man who ever lived and is arguably the richest person in history, writes, "One gives freely yet grows all the richer; another withholds what he should give, and only suffers want."

The late Zig Ziglar famously proclaimed, "You will get all you want in life, if you help enough other people get what they want."

I am a slow learner at times, but I am good at picking up patterns. The pattern that I discovered among these great men, what made them great, was their understanding of serving others. Their strength, wisdom, and experience empowered them to empower others. They made it their life mission to help others achieve their dreams, goals, and callings.

What Pastor Lee Armstrong showed me that February night in 2010 was "servant leadership." It wasn't something that he did or needed to be said. It's who he was. It's who he still is. He uses his time and energy to elevate others. He was a messenger from heaven that night. I needed him. I still do.

Thanks to that fateful night, I was on my way to serving others, too. My life was about to accelerate and climb to new heights, and it was going to be fueled by helping others.

Full of It

It may seem like an oxymoron at first. *"I'm going to exert energy to help someone else, and it is going to somehow make my dreams come true?"*

That's right! Imagine you have an empty balloon in your hand. For it to take shape, you need to inflate it. So, you place your mouth around the balloon. With one deep breath after another, you systematically fill the balloon to capacity. Winded and light-headed, but you did it. You quickly tie off the end to keep it from deflating, and there you have it, a fully inflated balloon.

What happens when you let go of the balloon? It drops to the ground, right? What if you filled the same balloon with helium and let go of it? It would fly away and eventually soar out of sight.

"Thanks for the obvious analogy! How profound of you," you might be thinking. Hang with me, there really is a powerful point that I am making.

Imagine your life is the balloon, and it is filled with ego. A life that is stretched to the max with self-consuming thoughts, actions, and self-preservation.

It's demoralizing and infuriating to be so exhausted only to stay at ground level. I don't know about you, but I am most unpleasant when I am tired and drained. Instead of being magnetizing, I become repulsive and people avoid me.

It doesn't have to be that way. It shouldn't be that way. Your life, like the balloon, needs to be filled with something different. When we ditch our ego, we make room for the new and begin to elevate.

The Apostle Paul, a first century missionary, contributed to nearly two-thirds of the writings in the Christian New Testament. Prior to his conversion to Christianity, he was a zealous religious leader who adamantly opposed the emerging movement of this new "Way."

History records that Saul (who would later have a name change to Paul) went from city to city to root out the followers of Jesus. He even oversaw the brutal killing of some. The primary issue that Saul and the others among the religious establishment had with this new "way" was that it threatened their ancient methodology and tradition. It was insulting their egos.

After all, if anyone deserved to have a blessed life, it was going to be the religious overachievers, right?

In one of Paul's letters to a group of Jesus-followers in Caesarea Philippi, he reveals the power that he gained by ditching his ego and receiving the new.

He writes in Philippians 3:4-10 (TPT),

> It's true that I once relied on all that I had become. I had a reason to boast and impress people with my accomplishments – more than others – for my pedigree was impeccable.
>
> I was born a true Hebrew of the heritage of Israel as the son of a Jewish man from the tribe of Benjamin. I was circumcised eight days after my birth and was raised in the strict

tradition of Orthodox Judaism, living a separated and devout life as a Pharisee. And concerning the righteousness of the Torah, no one surpassed me; I was without a peer. Furthermore, as a fiery defender of the truth, I persecuted the messianic believers with religious zeal.

Yet all of the accomplishments that I once took credit for, I've now forsaken them and I regard it all as nothing compared to the delight of experiencing Jesus Christ as my Lord! To truly know him meant letting go of everything from my past and throwing all my boasting on the garbage heap. It's all like a pile of manure to me now, so that I may be enriched in the reality of knowing Jesus Christ and embrace him as Lord in all of his greatness.

Tossed his Ego

My passion is to be consumed with him and not clinging to my own "righteousness" based in keeping the written Law. My "righteousness" will be his, based on the faithfulness of Jesus Christ – the very righteousness that comes from God. And I continually long to know the wonders of Jesus more fully and to experience the overflowing power of his resurrection working in me.

Trading "Me" for "We"

The Apostle Paul advanced the message of Jesus and Christianity further than any of his contemporaries. Arguably, he made the largest contribution to Christian Theology in modern history by saying that it was in the forsaking of everything that was only about *"me"* that led to experiencing overflowing power. Instead of holding on to all of his boast-worthy accomplishments, Saul let it go and found himself open-handed. A posture that was now ready to receive something new. Even a new name.

This *"something"* new as it turns out was *"Someone"* new, and He energized Paul to travel tens of thousands of miles and influence the known world. An influence that is still impacting millions of lives around the world today. Instead of tearing down, he learned the art of building people up. Something that he learned from Jesus.

You may be thinking, *"That sounds great if you're a minister or an apostle building churches, but how does this work in real life?"*

Great question that I believe can be answered in one word: principle. Principles are comprehensive and fundamental laws.

In other words, it works for everyone or it doesn't work for anyone. Principles cross geographical, racial, gender, and generational boundaries. The law of gravity, for example, takes none of these factors into consideration. If you jump out of a high-rise window or an airplane without a parachute, gravity will make sure that you hit the ground just like everyone else.

So, let's talk application.

CHAPTER 4

Less Hustle and More Humble

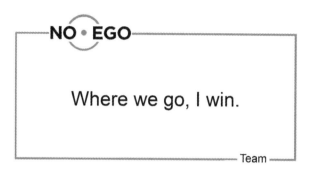

(*"If you're humble, you'll learn more. If you learn more, you'll earn more."* – Dr. Keith Johnson)

Get to Work!

I grew up in a family business. In every way imaginable. My family owned a small farm, an electrical contracting company, and a motorsports dealership. My step-father was a workaholic.

I discovered at a young age that if I wanted attention from him, it wasn't going to be by *"making the team"* or earning a lettermen's jacket. It was going to be by working. Working hard. Working a lot.

I began working for him when I was twelve. Well, I started getting paid when I was twelve. I received one dollar per hour. It was the summer of 1989. My parents had just purchased a different building to combine the electrical business with the motorsports business in one location. This was a massive project for us. The building was in rough shape and not set up for our desired layout.

At the end of my first week I remember sitting down with my mother and step-father. Mom had just printed off my very first paycheck when my step-dad had walked into her office space. I had never seen a business-sized check before.

I only had it in my hands for a few seconds before my step-dad asked to see it. He held it in his hands and looked at it with a mixture of surprise and approval. He looked back at me and paused before speaking, as if to indicate that this was important business. After what felt like minutes but was probably only a few seconds, he said, *"This is a lot of money."*

My head nervously nodded in agreement as he followed it up with a question that would haunt me most of my life. He asked, *"Did you work hard?"*

"Yes, sir," I replied.

His approving smile told me that I had finally found the *"thing"* that would make him proud of me. I learned that hustle meant approval and approval felt good. Really good.

I Make Bank

My first paycheck was for fifty-six dollars. That means I worked fifty-six hours that first week on payroll. It would turn out to be one of many fifty plus hour work weeks that summer as we prepared the building for its new purpose. I had never felt more valued or noticed by my step-dad than I did that summer. It was short-lived because in order to keep getting noticed, I had to keep ramping up my performance. A challenge that I was up for.

As I progressed into high school, instead of going on Christmas or Spring break trips like most of my friends, I took advantage to work forty or more hours if I could.

During my senior year of high school, I had the opportunity to work a Co-op program which allowed me to spend half of my day at school and work the other half for my parents. I worked whenever I could. I volunteered to come in early, stay late, and work Saturdays. Especially if it meant outworking or looking better than my step-brothers or other employees. I had found my jam, and I was good at it. I could outwork and outlast most anyone.

The day finally came when I felt that I was worth more than I was being paid. Though my hourly pay had progressed over the years, I was now married and had our first child. It was a matter of necessity, with a little bit of pride, too.

The conversation resulted in my two-week notice, followed by two months of my step-dad not speaking to me.

Rising to the Top
Just a few months prior to leaving my parents' business, I had attended a conference with speakers from all over the country. One speaker from Florida

was a pastor and author by the name of Sherman Owens. I had never heard of him nor have I ever heard anything of him since, but to this day I remember almost everything that man spoke. One of the nuggets he shared was, "No matter how big the pot, the cream always rises to the top."

This was valuable to me because I was leaving my parents' small business with just a handful of employees to join a 24/7 operation with hundreds of employees. So, I did what I always did. I worked. Really hard.

I was recognized within my first month as a standout. Supervisors and managers loved the kid who didn't know anything about the phrase, "That's not my job!"

Truth is, I didn't know any better. I came from a small family business and everything was "your job." I volunteered to come in early, work late, work weekends, and work holidays. Soon there was a job opening in the metallurgical lab. Something that I knew nothing about, but I knew it was better than the shop floor. I applied and got the position before my first sixty days. The position came with a pay increase and all the hours a guy could work. And so, I did.

More Please
This would become the pattern of my working life. I would make it my aim to outwork, outperform, and outlast anyone. It became an obsession. Something that I needed in order to feel valued. Something that I boasted about and dogged "slackers" as often as I could.

So long as the "atta boys" were coming and the incremental pay increases were being given, I felt successful. Something that I was not seeing or perhaps choosing to ignore was the strain this was causing my family and my health. I was rarely home, and when I was, I was still thinking about work.

When I would think about how little time I was giving my wife or kids, it made me feel like a failure. I hated feeling like I wasn't the best, so instead of addressing it, I stuck with what made me feel like a winner: working.

But it wasn't working anymore, and in order to face it, I had to ditch my ego.

Being a workaholic is not different than any other addiction. As with any addiction, you must keep increasing your dosage in order to receive your "high." There are only so many hours that a person can work. There are only so many family events that you can miss before there is irreparable damage to relationships.

The whole thing becomes a ticking time bomb ready to destroy everything you are attempting to build. It's hard to admit that you have reached your limit. Some don't admit it, and everything burns to ashes.

Way Out There

There is a great illustration found in the ancient Hebrew scriptures that I think is worth looking at. There is a famous account about a man by the name of Moses who is a sheepherder for his father-in-law, Jethro. These guys are so far out in the middle of nowhere that the script describes it as *"the backside of the desert."*

I don't know how far away from civilization you must be in order to be on the backside of the desert, but needless to say, they were WAY out there.

As the story goes, Moses is doing his thing, watching his sheep and looking out for danger. Something catches his eye; it's a small brush fire. Well, actually it's just one bush that is randomly on fire. That would puzzle me as well. Remember we are on the *"backside of nowhere!"*

If you're not familiar with the story, it says that Moses goes to investigate, but it wasn't the fact that the bush was on fire that got him so curious. Perhaps bushes spontaneously combust under the heat of the desert sun? I don't know.

So, what was it that got Moses's attention? It was the fact that the bush wasn't being consumed. The bush was on fire, but the fire wasn't burning up the bush.

As Moses gets just a little bit closer, he hears the voice of God speaking to him. For the rest of the story, you can check out Exodus chapter three, but for now I want to hover around this point. A point that may be as big of a game changer for you as it was for me.

Fire Retardant

We have already established that a random bush is burning in the middle of nowhere. Which by Moses's response must have happened from time to time. The intriguing thing to Moses was the fact that though the bush was burning, it wasn't burning up.

All this leads up to ... can you feel the suspense? Okay, here it is: "*Whatever God uses, He doesn't consume.*"

The opposite is true of us. We have limited resources, and if we rely on ability alone, we will eventually burn up. Our health, relationships, careers, and calling can all end in a pile of ashes. Is there a better way? You bet there is, but it will cost you. By now I am sure you've guessed what comes next? You need to ditch your ego.

To Be Clear

Before we move forward, I want to make sure to clearly state that I am in no way attempting to indicate that a strong work ethic is a bad thing. I am grateful for the work ethic that my step-dad instilled within me. It has served me well and opened many doors in my adult life.

However, for me it had become a matter of pride, and my work ethic had become my idol. My identity. Something that had to be protected, acknowledged, and be in the front-and-center on my stage of life. It was more important for me to be recognized for my work ethic than anything else. When people didn't do that, it was crushing for me.

In 2007, I had been given an opportunity that at the time was my dream job. I was hired by a Biotech company as an industrial maintenance mechanic. After only working in this role for six months, I was promoted to manager.

In this new role, my assignment was to build a trades department, later to be called "Plant Engineering."

The company was exploding with growth and had historically relied on outside contractors whenever repairs, equipment installation, and fabrication needs arose.

The cost of paying premium wages for contractors was part of the motivation to form this new department, but the real challenge was being held hostage to vendors' availability and time frames. It was becoming a bottleneck to the operation and beginning to hinder growth.

It was the biggest opportunity of my career, and I would soon learn that in order to succeed, I was going to have to ditch my ego. Let me explain.

Where We Go, I Win

Up to this point, my success and marketability was based on my abilities, expertise, and experience. In order to be a successful manager, I was going to have to assemble a diversified team with strengths and abilities that I didn't possess. In order to do that I was going to have to admit that I couldn't do it all.

This may seem obvious to you if you're successfully leading a team, but it was a scary concept for me. I had to let go of the map that got me to this point and lay hold of a whole new one that would guide me to future success. For the first time, my success was contingent on the team being successful. It was investing my energies into the crew that was going to produce increase in my life.

The easy part was creating a master list of tools, bins, cabinetry, and equipment to purchase. The real challenge was finding and hiring quality tradesmen. A technique that I learned from Bill Hybels's book, *Courageous Leadership,* served me well in this process.

In his book, he coined the phrase "The 3-Cs" which stand for Character, Competency, and Chemistry. Bill Hybels and his executive team used this method when adding staff or volunteers to teams. It was the filter that they funneled prospects through to identify quality candidates. They determined that if an individual was missing one of the "Cs," they were not the right fit for the team.

As I began to test this method, I found it to be incredibly helpful. I interviewed several people who had competency but lacked character or had both character and competency but no chemistry with the team.

As time went on, I hired a total of six tradesmen. I wish I could tell you that the "3-C" vetting process had a 100 percent success rate for me. Two of my hiring decisions ended up being real disappointments, but the other four were all-stars. Three are still with the company today, more than a decade later.

Dream Team

This was a *"dream team."* They were some of the most skilled, productive, motivated, and extra-mile effort guys I had ever worked with. One afternoon, I went to discuss some upcoming projects with them.

When I turned to leave, I noticed a small wooden plank had been hung over the door. On it was scribed, *"We may not have it all together, but together we have it all."*

It stopped me in my tracks. This wasn't a company-issued motivational poster. This was a custom-crafted piece of art that one of the guys hung as a reminder. This was a team-imposed, team-prescribed mission statement of the Plant Engineering Group.

It must have been my abrupt stop that got his attention. By the time I turned around, Matthew, one of my lead guys, was already smiling as our eyes locked. Before I could say anything, he said, "*Pretty much sums it up, doesn't it?*"

"*It sure does,*" I thought, but only nodded with a smile that matched his.

It wasn't long before I was promoted again and given even more responsibility. The company changed the organizational chart, and I was now reporting to the Vice President of the division. I was responsible for overseeing the maintenance, performance, and procurement of highly sophisticated automation and robotic equipment. I was also beginning to travel extensively throughout the United States and overseas in support of corporate acquisitions.

For me to be successful in this new role, I had to make sure my team was receiving the support they needed. This meant going to bat for them to receive above average pay increases. I kept meticulous records of repairs, fabrications, and cost savings that were realized by the ingenuity of my team.

There were several years in a row that Plant Engineering received the highest pay increases (in terms of percentages), more than any other department in the company. It also meant fighting for the budget to provide training, continued education, and courses for the team.

"What if you invest in these guys and they leave?" asked one executive at a budget meeting.

To which I replied, *"What if we don't and they stay?"*

That line item made the cut.

Winning

Learn the art of *"Celebrating Wins."* This is another game changer that I learned from Bill Hybels's book, *Courageous Leadership*. It's so simple that it is easy to overlook. Especially if you are "busy." Mr. Hybels writes, "What gets celebrated, gets repeated."

And boy is he right about this. It is as simple as recognizing a job well done, but it is most effective if it is done in front of others. Include the individual in an email to an affected manager who benefited from the job well done and praise the employee or volunteer. If you have the means, take them to lunch, give them a bonus, or nominate them for employee or volunteer of the month.

Keep It Real

I also discovered the more I poured into my team and made it my aim to elevate them, the more successful I became. I was rewarded handsomely by the company and acknowledged for the accomplishment of the department.

This should not be confused with flattery or a means to an end. When this is the case, it reveals our motive is still on self-preservation, and our ego is still in the driver's seat.

You may think you're fooling people, but they see right through the facade. Worse yet, it destroys trust, camaraderie, faithfulness, and loyalty. People will listen to you because they must, but they follow you because of trust.

CHAPTER 5

You Can Do It! Maybe?

NO • EGO

Success is less about talent, and more about preparedness.

Preparation

"Confidence without competence is a recipe for disaster." – Dr. Keith Johnson

Generationally Speaking

History would show that each generation can be attributed to amazing breakthroughs, advancements, and sociological milestones. It is also fair to say that there have been overcorrections, side effects, and extremes.

The pendulum swing from generation to generation has had distinct effects on morality, social norms, attitudes, activities, psychology, and ego.

Before we address a modern-day crisis, let's go back a few generations first and highlight a few definitive characteristics of these generations. My grandparents told me stories about living through The Great Depression. Their generation is sometimes referred to as the "GI Generation" or the "Greatest Generation." The suffering and memories of that time in American history would not be lost on them. Proof of that was easy to see by the way they lived their lives, purchases they made, and how they viewed money.

My grandfather was a successful man who proudly served his country in the United States Navy. He met my grandmother on the train to boot camp and married her shortly after. They started a family quickly, and after completing his stint in the Navy, he went to work to support his family. He knew that he wanted more for his family than what being a security guard at a factory could offer him. So, at twenty-eight years old, with a wife, two children, and a full-time job, he enrolled in college. He finished his degree and went to work for the State of Michigan, where he spent more than thirty years before retiring. Something that he would remind me routinely in my early adulthood.

My grandparents' generation had a mistrust of the banking institution and worried about the economy. By and large, they were not risk takers and had minimal debt. They went to work for one company and remained there until retirement. Wives rarely worked outside the home. They took great pride in maintaining the home, raising the children, and supporting their husbands. A home-cooked family meal was where the family gathered every evening.

In the Midwest in the 1950s and 1960s, where my grandparents were raising their family, families lived simply and modestly. Clothing was often hand-made, repaired, or patched when damaged, and handed down to younger siblings. Family vacations were something they saved up for and were usually destinations that could be driven to.

Booming

The Baby Boomers were going to approach life much differently. Boomers inherited a strong work ethic from their parents and aren't afraid to put in a hard day of work. For many of this generation, their self-worth comes directly from their professional achievements. They acknowledge that success comes from dedicating a great deal of time and effort into their careers, which also means that they may find it difficult to find the perfect home-work balance.

The feminist movement of the 1960s and '70s originally focused on dismantling workplace inequality, such as denial of access to better jobs and salary inequity, via anti-discrimination laws. As such, the different wings of the feminist movement sought women's equality on both a political and personal level. The status quo of "the woman's place is in the home" was dismantled.

This Boomer generation is independent, self-assured, competitive, and goal-oriented. One of their biggest motivators is racing to the top of the corporate ladder, or a leaderboard doing their best to surpass their peers and co-workers. One of the baby boomers' strongest characteristics is their strong sense of community. They thrive in team environments. Additionally, baby boomers like structure. Many grew up in households that were highly disciplined and structured, which shaped who they are today.

This is also the generation that welcomed rock and roll, civil rights, television, and credit cards. They pushed at traditional boundaries and social norms.

Due to the sheer size of their generation, these shifts caused substantial change. This rebellious streak extended to relationships, marriage, and families as well. When we look at divorce by generation, the most drastic shift occurs here. Also known as the "Me Generation," large slices of the population began to put individual fulfillment ahead of traditional family roles.

This holds true today. Baby Boomers continue to divorce more than any other age group. In the years between 1990 and 2012, the divorce rate for people aged fifty-five to sixty-four doubled. For those older than sixty-five, that number more than tripled.

Small Package, Big Footprint

Generation X became the influencers of its younger and older generations. What they lack in numbers (just 66 million to boomers' 75 million), they make up with ingenuity, development, corporate success, and business.

For a small and supposedly lost generation, they have found their way to positions of power. A staggering fifty-five percent are part of Generation X. X'ers are also among the most highly educated generation in the U.S.: thirty-five percent have college degrees vs. nineteen percent of Millennials.

They're tech savvy, much like Millennials, and they know how to use social media with ease: Eighty-one percent of Gen X is on Facebook and 5.9 million have Snapchat accounts. But they engage with their online identities less for selfie-centered promotion and more to keep up with current affairs — and reach their Millennial kids (on Snapchat).

It used to be a given that one generation would learn, take the baton, and carry it further than the previous generation, but not so with Generation X. Although they have purchasing power (thirty-one percent of U.S. income, but just twenty-five percent of the population), they have less wealth than their parents did at their age twenty-five years ago. This is partially due to overwhelming college debts.

The boomers raised Gen X'ers, generally speaking, not lacking for much. The Boomers, who were raised modestly, did not raise X'ers the same way.

In comparison, Gen X'ers were raised in extravagance compared to their parents, and a new bar of "normal" was established. What may have taken boomers decades to establish, Generation X expected to have immediately. So, like their parents, they borrowed. And they spend nearly everything they make.

That's Not How I Did It When I Was Your Age

There is a lot being said and published about Millennials these days, and for good reason. Studies show that the Millennials will surpass the boomer generation in population by the end of 2019. This generation of people born between 1981 and 1996 represent more than twenty percent of the U.S. population and are the modern-day workforce. Their approach to life is very different than previous generations, due in large part to the internet and rapidly advancing technology.

I want to be quick to point out that "*different*" should not be implied as "*bad.*" At least not in every case. It is my opinion that one of the greatest attributes of the Millennials is that they challenge status quo.

Millennials love music, creativity, and care about social causes. Much like the Boomers, they question authority and ask "*Why?*" more than a three-year-old. They demand explanations and will fact check you in mid-conversation by simply "*Googling*" it.

They are also highly educated. In fact, they are the most educated generation in history, with over twenty-three percent holding a bachelor's degree or higher. The Millennials' version of the American Dream is unlike previous generations, and their path is different, too.

Their version of the American Dream, in large part, is not going to be obtained by the sweat of their brow. That is not to say that they aren't going to work hard. They're just going to question the method and likely approach it more streamlined. Relating to Millennials has been a struggle for Boomers and Generation X'ers. Sometimes these previous generations even label Millennials as lazy. Is it lazy or just finding another way?

Some additional distinctions about the Millennials is that they are not as car crazed as previous generations. Many even put off obtaining a driver's license until adulthood or not at all, opting for car sharing services like Uber or Lyft to avoid the overhead and maintenance of car ownership.

Speaking of ownership, the Millennials are abandoning suburban life and flocking to cities. For the first time since the 1920s, growth in U.S. cities outpaces the growth outside of the cities. All of this and more is creating a cultural shift and way of life. Statistics show that the shift is also producing the most stressed group in history.

Bumming Me Out

According to the American Psychological Association, twelve percent of Millennials have an officially diagnosed anxiety disorder. This is almost double the percentage of baby boomers. Additional studies have found that thirty percent of working Millennials are classified with general anxiety, and a 2014 American College Health Association (ACHA) assessment found that sixty-one percent of college students experience frequent anxiety.

Millennials undoubtedly experience a great deal of stress, and subsequently, difficulty properly managing it. This is a generational crisis.

Technology overload has been said to be a common leading cause of increased feelings of anxiety, social isolation, and stress – yet many people still cling to it. A 2015 study reported by *Time* found that Americans aged twenty-five to thirty-four check their devices on average fifty times per day, and those aged thirty-five to forty-four roughly thirty-five times daily.

Tech Crunch estimated in 2017 that, collectively, adults spend about five hours daily on mobile devices.

Being overly reliant on technology has been shown to escalate central nervous system arousal, in turn increasing anxiety while decreasing mood.

I Thought We Were Friends

A large segment of the Millennial population has never known life without the worldwide web, cellular and wirelesses devices, or social media. This has provided a source of connection and confidence that is both fraudulent and crippling.

How so? Inherently we understand friends to be a person who you know, who knows you, and whom you have a bond of mutual affection. An expectation is created in our minds that this person is important and so is their opinion.

When we have hundreds or thousands of *"friends"* on our social media platforms, it can damage our self-worth, our ego, and destroy our confidence if we come up short on the likes, hearts, and thumbs-ups. Conversely, it can also bring a false sense of approval and a confidence that is not founded in competency. As Dr. Johnson said, *"Confidence without competency is a recipe for disaster."*

When I woke up Tuesday, September 11, 2001, I thought it was like any other morning. That would change as soon as I turned on the television. It had only been a few minutes since American Airlines Flight 11 had crashed into the North Tower (1 WTC) of the World Trade Center. It didn't compute with my still partially asleep mind as to what I was seeing. It looked like the scene of a movie or a commercial for a new movie? It was too fantastical to be real.

"Wait ... where did they say this was?" I thought as I leaned toward the television. New York City! I was glued to the emergency news broadcast when Flight 175 crashed into the South Tower (2 WTC) of the World Trade Center. It was unimaginable.

I had never experienced anything as horrifying as what I was seeing. I was stunned and shocked. America was filled with shock. Along with fear, anger, and patriotism. Tens of thousands of young men and woman enlisted in the military in response to the worst terrorist attack on the soil of the U.S.

Preparation
Imagine if the military received the influx of confident young men and woman and immediately dispatched them into combat. No basic training. No physical fitness. No specialized training. But full of patriotic zeal, concern, and confidence.

These are motivators to get us activated and keep us committed but are not the tools that will assure our success. Attempting to learn combat skills and proper use of a weapon while under fire, under attack, and pressured from every side would not only put your life at risk but the lives of the soldiers around you.

Perhaps a battle scene is too exaggerated or extreme of an example to relate to your environment. After all, it's not like we're taking on enemy fire from the cubicle down the row. However, our success and the success of others depends on our competency.

Success is rarely an issue of talent. It is most often an issue of preparedness.

Two Sides of the Same Coin

I want to affirm that I believe confidence is vital to our success, but it must be established on skillset. Conversely, we can have all the skill in the world, but if we lack confidence, we will never execute.

Andrew Wommack, International Minister and founder of Charis Bible College, uses the illustration of sodium and chloride to make a similar point. Sodium, if consumed, is poison. And if the right amount is ingested, it is deadly. The same is true with chloride. Chloride, if consumed, is poison. And, like sodium, it is deadly if consumed.

However, magic happens when you combine the two elements. Sodium-Chloride becomes common table salt, and without salt – you will die.

Confidence and competence are two sides of the same coin. Combined, they are the key to obtaining your dream.

I have discovered that authentic confidence, built on skillset, is a process that takes time, commitment, and humility. Something the ego will resist. Repetition is necessary to achieving success.

Thomas Edison, inventor of the light bulb, is said to have had ten thousand failed attempts before creating a functioning bulb. His response was, *"I have not failed. I've just found 10,000 ways that won't work."*

How many times do we quit after one failed attempt? It is ego that says we must get it right every time, the first time. That's not real life! Failure is not the opposite of success; it is part of the equation.

Nelson Mandela once said, *"I never lose. I either win or learn."*

Knowledge is power because it provides the ability to perform better, serve more, create more, and provide solutions. Ego puts on a façade of confidence and will exhaust itself attempting to convince everyone that it has the goods. Whereas authentic confidence not only allows results to speak for themselves, it makes its objective to assist others to achieve their goals, too.

What's the Rush?

We live in a "drive-thru" society that demands convenience. We expect a quality product, delivered fast with minimal disruption to our schedule – and cheap! This mindset has crept into many aspects of our lives, and the unfortunate reality is that a "microwave mentality" is not going to serve up the future of your dreams.

Developing competency is more of a crock-pot or slow cooker approach. In Malcolm Gladwell's book *Outliers*, he introduces the idea of the 10,000-hour rule. The principle holds that ten-thousand hours of deliberate practice are needed to become world-class in any field.

Gladwell uses the seemingly overnight success of the Beatles to illustrate his point. The band's UK breakout year came in 1962, and their popularity spread to the U.S. A few weeks prior to the band's first visit to America, their hit single, "I Want to Hold Your Hand," sold one and a half million copies in under three weeks. When the Beatles landed in New York City in February 1964, they were greeted by five thousand fans and more than two hundred reporters. They were an overnight sensation. Or were they?

Gladwell's research for *Outliers* reveals some history about the Beatles that many are not aware of. Gladwell writes,

> "The Beatles had a musical gift, but what made them the Beatles was a random invitation to play in Hamburg ... where they performed live as much as five hours a night, seven days a week. Talented? Absolutely," he says. "But they also simply put in more hours than anyone else. On the first trip, they played 106 nights, five or more hours a night," he writes. "On their second trip, they played 92 times. On their third trip, they played 48 times, for a total of 172 hours on stage. The last two Hamburg gigs, in November and December of 1962, involved another 90 hours of performing. All told, they performed 270 nights in just over a year and a half. By the time they had their first burst of success in 1964, in fact, they had performed live an estimated twelve hundred times. Do you know how extraordinary that is? Most bands today don't perform twelve hundred times in their entire careers."

You Got to Keep It Marinated

To grow in confidence and competence will require us to fully immerse. To marinate. My oldest son and I love to grill steak, and we have fun coming up with unique marinades. He is more creative with his marinade concoctions than I am, but I am more patient when it comes to letting them bathe.

What I have discovered is that the longer the steak soaks in the sauce, the deeper the flavor penetrates the meat. A quick dip or splash on your steak may provide you with a hint of flavor, but once you get past the surface, the flavor is lost.

In order to have depth and resources to draw from in challenging times, you need to be immersed in your craft. When the pressure is applied, it will reveal what is inside. Does your label match the content? When squeezed, I want solutions revealed, not my ego.

Everyone Needs a Coach

Coach John Wooden was the first person to be inducted into the Basketball Hall of Fame both as a player and coach. ESPN ranks him as the greatest coach of all time, across all sports. He led his UCLA men's basketball team to a stunning ten NCAA Championships in twelve years. Coach Wooden famously said, *"Peace of mind is attained only through self-satisfaction in knowing you made the effort to do the best of which you're capable."*

Coaches have an ability to identify potential and help us maximize our performance. Coaching is more about helping someone to learn than teaching them. Wooden promoted the idea of a *"teacher-coach."*

It is no coincidence that the highest performing athletes and executives alike have coaches. During an April 2013 TED Talk, Bill Gates, the founder of Microsoft and second richest person on the planet, opened his talk with *"Everyone needs a coach."* He would go on to say, *"We all need people who will give us feedback. That is how we improve."*

We all need someone who can watch what we do and give us their perspective. The one thing that people are never good at is seeing themselves as others see them.

Tom Landry, who coached the Dallas Cowboys for twenty-nine seasons said, *"A coach is someone who tells you what you don't want to hear, who has you see what you don't want to see, so you can be who you have always known you could be."*

If we're serious about achieving our goals and dreams and becoming the very best version of ourselves, then we need to ditch our ego and find a coach.

CHAPTER 6

Dreamy

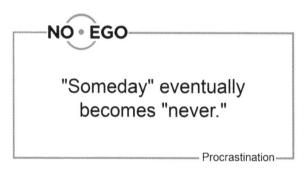

NO • EGO

"Someday" eventually
becomes "never."

Procrastination

"Vision without action is merely a dream."
— Joel H. Barker

I Struggle with Dreamers

Recently I had to make a day trip, and I asked my son to take the ride with me. We generally have great conversations, but this trip was one that I will remember for years. I am very fortunate to have the type of connection with my children that allows for honesty and transparency. The established level of trust and support that has been built over time leads to deep, authentic, and rich conversations. Conversations that include admitting areas of faults and failures in our lives.

I enjoy talking with my boys about growth-minded actions and future endeavors. I want them to grow up thinking like "owners" and to never put their futures in the hands of someone else. To be ones who take accountability, take responsibility, and act. The conversation led me to admit, "I struggle with most dreamers."

He was puzzled. And maybe you are, too.

I went on to explain. "It's not that I am not interested in people's dreams and aspirations. I am. But I am far more interested in hearing about what they're currently working on to get closer to achieving their dream."

You see, I am an encourager to the core. I am wired by God to assume the best about people, and I have an eye for potential. I get as excited about what others are building as much as I do about what I am working on. I am really interested in people's success, and I am always investigating what people are doing so I can get excited with them. It comes natural for me.

But I have noticed that my tolerance isn't what it used to be when it comes to expressed ideas, goals, dreams, and passions. I want to see action!

A Little More Action

Let's return to the conversation my son and I were having in the car. Isiac, my son, wanted further explanation to my statement because it seemed like a contradiction to him. In his estimation, his dad is a dreamer.

So, I went on to explain that I was worn out on lofty talk, heated emotional moments, and temporary inspiration. For me, this ranged from conversations with friends, acquaintances, and strangers to emotional sermons and motivational speakers. If it didn't involve demonstrated success, implemented action plans, or at the very least a next step – I tune out quickly. No more rhetoric. No more clichés. No more "We're about to." Sorry, no more patience.

By this point, Isiac is nodding in agreement but squinting his eyes as if he is still trying to track with me.

Recognizing that further explanation was needed I said, "Basically son, I just want a person's actions to speak louder than their words. I don't want to hear about it unless you're doing it or about to do it." I continued with, "I know that there is an element to dreaming and expanding our imagination and ideas of what is possible. I admit that I could do better at that."

Just then Isiac interrupted me and blurted out, "But that is what I love about you!"

My first thought was that he was complimenting me about admitting an area that I could improve on, but that was not where he was going. What he said next meant the world to me.

Private Jets

He said, "What I have learned about you, Dad, is that if you're talking about it, it's going to happen."

His eyes popped open a little wider as examples came to mind. After a short pause, he continued, "Like when you and Mom were talking about getting a boat, I knew we were getting a boat. And even though you have not come right out and said it, I already know it's *a matter of time before you buy the Audi you keep pointing out."*

We shared a smile because we both knew he was right.

"But you really freaked me out the other night!" he exclaimed.

"Really, how?" I asked.

He said, *"Remember when we were hanging out, and you were scrolling through Instagram looking at private jets?"*

I didn't say anything. I just nodded and anxiously waited for the rest of what he had to say.

Isiac fell back into the passenger seat and said, *"All I could think was 'Holy Cow, we're getting a private jet!'"*

You see, my son had become so accustomed to actions following my words, he thought that the fact that I was looking at images of jets and showing him pictures of ones that I thought were super cool, meant we were in the market. For the record, I am not, but I love that this was his knee-jerk response!

Maybe it's semantics, but I make a distinction between visionaries and dreamers. Visionaries, to me, can see what is possible and implement a plan to achieve it. Emphasis being on *"implementation."*

Ego is one of the primary reasons we put off implementation and continue to use phrases that begin with:

"When I…"

"I'm going to…"

"Then I…"

All this does is cast our dreams into the future.

Someday

Eventually, someday becomes never. It's a distraction method. In order to distract us from our lack of action, we find something new to fantasize about. We need the rush of emotion, excitement, and thrill of what could be because it numbs the pain of our reality.

The ego needs to protect its image and guard its persona. In order to masquerade the truth, we develop a great story about what we are going to do. The story is usually pretty good and gets people pumped for you. The tragedy of it all is when we begin to believe our story and convince ourselves that the fantasy is reality. The wake-up call is jarring, humiliating, and expensive.

But it doesn't have to be this way anymore. Ditch your ego and find your plan.

There are fewer things worse than a person who loses confidence in themselves. A sure sign of this is when your internal dialect is on "repeat" and reminds you of all the times you failed to follow through. Once self-confidence is lost, our identity is next. We begin to believe that this is who we are instead of what we did. The story we believe is the life that we will get.

What if I told you that rewriting the story was not only possible but simple? Simple doesn't always mean easy. You still must participate.

Like Harley Davidson once said, *"When writing the story of your life, don't let anyone else hold the pen."*

We're talking about regaining confidence, changing your internal story, shifting momentum, and becoming a visionary.

It Can Be Regained

You have arrived at your current condition (mentally and physically) due to a blend of decisions and experiences. The good news is, if you don't like the experiences you had up to this point, all you need to do is make different decisions.

"How profound! Thank you for this deep revelation," you may be thinking, as you roll your eyes. Stick with me just a little longer. I'm going someplace with this.

It is easy for us to get intimidated because we link decisions with discipline, and if we had discipline, we would already be experiencing more of what we desire. What we neglect to remember is that discipline is like a muscle that must be strengthened. I may want to step into the gym and bench press three hundred pounds like I did when I was thirty, but if I get under a barbell with that kind of weight after being absent from the gym for more than a decade, it is going to be a disaster! I wholeheartedly believe I could do it again, but I am going to have to take some steps to build the muscle. The same is true with building discipline.

My first suggestion is so simple that it is easy to reject, but I wouldn't dismiss the value of subtle changes to make big improvement.

You ready for this? Begin with your alarm clock.

"My alarm clock is going to help me regain confidence?"

That's right! I will share my wake-up time, but I am not implying that you need to do the same or begin with this time. I didn't. I realized that if I wanted to accomplish more, I needed more time to work.

My most productive and creative time is the morning hours, so I began waking myself up at 5:00 AM. The time is relative to your schedule and personal needs. For the sake of this conversation, I will say that the time is less the point, and more about you responding to it.

Morning person or not, when that alarm goes off at 5:00 AM, it is difficult to leave the comfort of my nice, warm bed with my beautiful wife lying next to me.

I'm going to be honest with you. At the beginning, I hit the snooze bar. A lot. That is until I read Mel Robbins's book, *The 5 Second Rule*. This one nugget literally changed my life.

Get Up!

Robbins's book is loaded with great advice and encouragement, but it was her insight on sleep cycles that revolutionized my life. According to research, we experience sleep cycles throughout the night. Each cycle is between sixty and ninety minutes. Depending on how long we sleep, the average person will go through three or four cycles each night.

The final cycle is preparing you to come out of your comatose state. When the alarm clock wakes you up, and you decide to snooze it rather than get up, you enter another sleep cycle ... one that requires sixty to ninety minutes to complete.

When the temporarily delayed alarm goes off again, it wakes you from an incomplete sleep cycle, and the crippling effect is felt for half the day. As it turns out, it takes four to six hours to recover from a broken sleep cycle.

Have you ever had one of those days where you just can't seem to wake up? It doesn't matter that you have coffee hooked up like an I.V., you just can't snap out of it. We thought a couple more minutes in bed was going to be the boost we needed, but instead it was self-sabotage. I had to put this to the test.

You've Got Five Seconds to Figure It Out

One Sunday morning when the alarm went off at 5:00 AM, I could hear Mel's voice in my head saying, "5,4,3,2,1 Get up!" And I did.

The first five to seven minutes were as unpleasant as one might expect, but I was up and moving. At the time, the church that I pastor was offering four Sunday morning service times, and it was incredibly draining on me. I would leave church exhausted and in desperate need of a nap. But not this day. It didn't occur to me at first, but I had successfully delivered my message four different times, made it home, and felt surprisingly alert.

"Could it really be the Five Second Rule that made the difference?" I thought with skepticism.

I decided to repeat the practice again on Monday morning. Alarm sounds off at 5:00 AM, "5,4,3,2,1 Get up!" I repeated in my head and jumped out of bed. Remarkably, I felt more energized the entire day just like the day before.

I share this tip with as many people as I can because of the profound effect it has had on my energy level. At first it was a necessary evil to obtaining my goals, but what I discovered was it became the pace car for the rest of my day. I had already made and kept my first commitment. I decided to wake up at a designated time, and I followed through. I had taken control. I was taking charge of my schedule. I began my mornings with intentionality, and momentum was beginning to build.

The story was starting to change. My confidence was being established. When I say I am going to do something, I do it!

Momentum is difficult to get started and yet easy to maintain. But it must be maintained. Have you ever had to push a car that had stalled? When my wife Becky and I got married, we really struggled financially. I think we went through three different cars that first year. We could only afford a few hundred-dollar car, and they were prone to frequent breakdowns.

We began to think there was a plot against us, as the cars conveniently waited to stall at intersections or stoplights. Or at rush hour. The drivers behind us often interpreted the breakdown as a calculated effort to ruin their lives. At least that is what we gathered by the honking, screaming, and profanities.

We had the routine down, and we would jump into action, pushing the car out of the middle of the busy intersection and into the closest lot. The initial effort of getting the car moving was hard, but once we had momentum, we pushed the car with little effort.

I'm Really Doing It!

Regaining and maintaining self-confidence is done by continued simple decisions. Remember, subtle changes make for big improvements. The act of creating a daily schedule and sticking to it is another act of control. Keeping appointment times is another tool to regaining and maintaining self-confidence.

It is a form of keeping your word, and when you give your word, you follow through. It is more important to focus on moving forward than it is the size of your steps.

The act of creating a schedule and sticking to it is also a form of goal-setting. When you establish quantifiable goals with deadlines, you begin to see progress.

Progress is the key to happiness. Progress shifts our expectation. Hope is a form of expectation. Hope is an expectation of good. We begin to expect good results because our story is filled with new experiences. Experiences that confirm that I am indeed a visionary. A builder. A producer. A winner.

It's a Campaign

Getting better is not a *"hack."* Getting better is a campaign. There is no magic pill, secret, one-time investment, or luck. Like Oprah Winfrey says, *"I do not believe in luck. I believe that success comes when preparation and opportunity meet."*

It requires daily focus and determination. Both of which will be regularly challenged. There is a reason why race horses wear blinders. Horses have peripheral vision, which means they can end up running off course unless they are made to remain focused on what is ahead of them. Blinders are small squares of firm leather that attach to the bridle at the side of the horse's head.

We must stay focused on the finish line as well if we want to stay on course. The best way to stay focused is to ditch your ego. Let me explain.

Along the race track there are grandstands filled with spectators. Some are cheering, and some are booing! The same is true in life. You'll have fans that will cheer and bet on you to win, but you'll have naysayers, too. Many of which are well-meaning friends and family who think that they are "helping you" to think responsibly, rationally, and reasonably.

The so-called advice is usually rooted in their own insecurity, and your success threatens their ego. The antagonism will be personal, and if you don't ditch your ego, you'll lose focus.

Stay the Course

Imagine you are a runner in a race and someone in the grandstand begins heckling you. What they are saying about you is wrong and inaccurate, so you run into the stands to set them straight.

After all, what if the people around the heckler believed what they were saying? You may deliver the most persuasive argument and set that person in their place. You stand justified before all the other fans who witnessed the injustice done to your good name. You win!

Or did you? You may have won the argument, but you left the race. You got off course.

Why? Ego. If the opinion of others means more to you than staying on course, you will leave the race every time someone speaks unfairly about you.

If you do that enough times, you'll lose the race. Just keep running.

Desperate People Do Desperate Things

Sticking with the race theme, let's look at another scenario. What if you are outpacing another runner, and in a desperate attempt to gain the lead, they trip you. Desperation, insecurity, and ego provokes people to do and say some extremely mean things.

Have you ever been tripped up by somebody simply because you were getting good results? You're not alone. When you decide to take charge of your life, you begin to separate from the pack that once camouflaged you. You stand out. You become noticed. You become an easier target.

When someone does or says something cruel to you, it says far more about them than it does you. We cannot control what others do, but we can control our response.

Revenge or Success?

On several occasions I have had lies said about me, social media attacks, and rumors spread. Some are laughable, but others cut deep.

The attacks that hurt the most are from the ones you have poured your life into. Betrayal can be the most difficult assault to recover from. But you must. You have a race to run. A course to finish. A dream to be accomplished. Resist the temptation to retaliate. You don't have time or energy to waste on getting revenge.

Ego demands retribution, and you need to decide — do you want revenge or success? Frank Sinatra said it best, "*The best revenge is massive success.*"

Ditch your ego, find your pace, and finish the race.

CHAPTER 7

Who Are You?

NO • EGO

Failure is your friend,
not your foe.

———— Becoming

"You cannot know every challenge you will face, but you can know who you are when you face that challenge." – Erwin McManus

If at First You Don't Succeed

History is filled with accomplished inventors, writers, dignitaries, industry moguls, and athletes. Names like Edison, Rowling, Churchill, Ford, and Jordan are all associated with greatness. Their contribution to society has made them celebrated history makers and household names.

What doesn't always make the highlight reels are the challenges they faced and overcame before anyone ever knew their name.

The fact that you're reading this book is an indicator that you have big dreams and aspirations of greatness. And you should because you have greatness in you. The road to greatness is hard, uncomfortable, and peppered with failures and several disappointments. Nobody has it easy. Including the names I listed above.

I used to be intrigued with accomplished individuals in any sphere of life, but now I am infatuated with learning about their journey. I have learned that success leaves clues. The more I study the process of success, the more I respect those who build or accomplish great things.

As a result, I better understand their struggles, endurance, and preparation. If we don't study their stories, we may miss their greatest contribution of all. The history-makers didn't live their lives waiting for the great moment to come, instead they lived their lives preparing for it.

I already mentioned Edison earlier in the book, but it is worth sharing again. As the story goes, a reporter interviewing Thomas Edison about his invention of the light bulb asked Mr. Edison, *"How did you keep from giving up when you failed 10,000 times in your effort to invent the light bulb?"*

"I never failed. I simply found 10,000 ways that did not work," Edison replied with a smile.

Winston Churchill, on the day that he fulfilled his life's ambition of becoming Britain's Prime Minister, Germany had that very morning invaded France, Belgium, the Netherlands, and Luxembourg. Britain faced its supreme test. Churchill would later write, *"I felt ... that all my past life had been but a preparation for this hour and for this trial."*

It is for his leadership through Dunkirk, the lengthy Battle of Britain, and the Blitz that Churchill is best remembered.

Not an Overnight Success Story

J.K. Rowling had the idea for Harry Potter in 1990. Later that same year she lost her mother. In 1992, she moved to Portugal to teach English where she met a man, got married, and had a daughter. The marriage ended in 1993. Now a single mom, she moved back to England to be closer to family.

Rowling was broke, fighting depression, and living on government assistance. After completing her book in 1995, she was rejected by twelve publishers. Finally, in 1996, she convinced a small publishing house to print her book. In 1997, the book was published with only a thousand copies, five hundred of which were distributed to libraries. In 1997 and 1998, the book won awards from Nestle Smarties Book Prize and the British Book Award for Children's Book of the Year. After that, it was one wild ride for Rowling.

Today, Rowling has sold more than four hundred million copies of her books and is one of the most successful authors of all time.

Ford Motor Company is one of the most successful automotive companies in the world, but its founder, Henry Ford, failed at two previous attempts. Both resulting in bankruptcies. Instead of giving up, Ford learned from the process, stating, *"Failure is simply the* opportunity to begin again, this time more intelligently."

Failure to Mr. Ford was simply part of the equation, not the end. He revolutionized the automobile industry, introducing not only the Model T and the assembly line, but also the concept of an automobile for every home. Driving became the new form of transportation, and subsequently, Ford's Model T went on to sell over 17 million units.

Michael Jordan, considered by many to be the best professional basketball player of all time (sorry Lebron fans), understood the value of responding to failure correctly. In 2006, Nike aired the now famous "Failed" commercial. The thirty-second commercial features Jordan in a slow-motion walk making his way to a player's entrance. The narration is done by Jordan himself as he reflects on his career:

> "I've missed more than 9000 shots in my career. I've lost almost 300 games. 26 times I've been trusted to take the game winning shot ... and missed. I've failed over and over and over again in my life. And that is why I succeed."

When No One Knows Your Name – Yet!

Larry Bird is perhaps the best example when it comes to preparing for the big moment. Bird is one of the best players ever to play basketball, which is why he is in the Basketball Hall of Fame. He was especially good at shooting, particularly free throws.

In the history of the NBA, there are only four free throw shooters who rank higher than Bird. In thirteen years, he made eighty-nine percent of his free throws.

Bird grew up in French Lick, Indiana. Ever heard of it? Me neither. He used to refer to himself as *"The Hick from French Lick."* When he was in high school, he would get out of bed early so he could walk to school and practice his free throws in the gym. Bird said that in high school he would shoot five hundred free throws every morning before his first class.

Hard work paid off for Larry, and it will pay off for you … because hard work always does. Our willingness to work hard in obscurity will greatly impact our future visibility. The fear that many of us contend with in the early stages of preparation is that we'll never be noticed. We talk ourselves out of putting in the work and look for shortcuts. Some of the best advice I have ever heard about preparation came from the late Jim Rohn.

If You Will Change, Everything Will Change

Rohn was one of the leading motivational speakers of the 20th Century. He was a brilliant storyteller who commonly used his own journey to illustrate his points. He speaks about his mentor, Earl Shoaff, but always as "Mr. Shoaff" in his stories.

He met Mr. Shoaff when he was twenty-five years old, and as Jim tells the story, "Mr. Shoaff said to me, 'Mr. Rohn, if you will change, everything else will change.'"

Over the next five years, Rohn began to implement the instruction of his new mentor, and by the time Jim was thirty years old, he was a millionaire.

The lesson that I learned from Mr. Rohn that has had profound implications in my life is this: "*Success is not something that you pursue. Success is what you attract by the person you become. Your life will not get better by chance; it will get better by change. And if you will change, everything will change.*"

I'll Pass

The process of preparation is about becoming more, not just doing more. To view the process as a necessary evil or as a means to an end is to miss the value altogether. How many times did we cram for a test or memorize answers in order to score well on an exam?

This was routine for me growing up. I memorized answers to questions, but that didn't mean I learned the material. The system rewarded me for doing so. I received passing grades from my teachers and "atta-boys" from my parents.

As an ultimate prize, I was graduated to the next grade. This is the case for many students, and the tragedy is that it programs the student to do only what is required to pass. When "*passing*" becomes the target instead of "*excelling*," we get lost in the sea of mediocrity.

The measure of our value is reduced to percentiles, and as long as we are consistent with the average – we're good. Only mediocre mindsets think in terms of average income, weight, debt, education, and a retirement plan. When you settle for average, you are just as close to the bottom as you are the top. Let that sink in.

We should never measure our success based on how well we compare to others. Imagine your child comes home from school and boasts about receiving the highest grade out of the entire class on the last test. What parent wouldn't be excited? The natural question would be to ask, "What did you get on the test?"

Your child responds with, "I got 48!"

Still feeding off the enthusiasm of your child, you smile and ask, "48 out of what, sweetie?"

You are anticipating 48 out of 48 or even 48 out of 49 if they got the highest grade in the class. Right?

And then they tell you, "48 out of 100."

That means your child failed, even though they did better than all the other students.

You're Amazing

There is nothing average about you. The ancient Hebrew Scriptures refer to you as "wonderfully and fearfully made." You are a miracle. You are one out of forty million sperm that made it to the egg. You've been great from the beginning. You are wired for greatness but have been programed for average.

You will never be content being camouflaged by the masses. It's true that you have potential, but potential alone is not enough. Let's return to Jim Rohn's story again before we go any further.

Two Types of People

As mentioned earlier in the chapter, Jim spent five years being mentored by Mr. Shoaff and successfully became a millionaire by the time he was thirty years old. The more remarkable part of his story is that he was broke by the time he was thirty-two.

How is that remarkable? That just sounds sad, right? It would be if that is how the story ended. Rohn had never been exposed to the level of income he was generating and made the same mistake that many of us make. We adjust our lifestyle to match our income. We stop asking *"How much?"* and start asking *"How many colors does it come in?"*

As a result, Jim had failed to retain his wealth, but failing is not the same as losing. This was a concept that I struggled with for years. I have heard it said that we *"fail our way to success,"* but it never made sense to me.

Maybe you're thinking the same thing. Isn't failure the opposite of success? No, failure is part of the process. Les Brown says, *"There are two types of people in this world. Winners and those who haven't figured out how to win yet."*

Embracing the process is vitally important to obtaining your goals and dreams, but the real value is what you become in the process. After losing his first million, Rohn said, *"It's a good thing that I am a millionaire!"*

Wait, the man just lost his fortune. He isn't even a "thousand-aire" let alone a millionaire! Mr. Rohn was grateful for the process because the process had taught him how to earn millions. The failure taught him what to do differently with the money when he earned it again. And he did. Many times over.

Failure is not the end. It only becomes the end if we quit. Failure simply reveals your current limitation.

Failure Is Your Friend

In the exercise and fitness world, the term *"failure"* is often used as a goal. You do as many reps with a weight as you can until you fail to lift it one more time. One morning years ago, my workout partner and I were bench pressing until "failure." Each time we reached our limit, we quickly removed some of the weight from the bar and kept on pressing. We did this until we were just lifting the bar. If you had arrived at the gym at the end of our workout, it would have been comical to witness a physically fit man red faced, shaking, and groaning to lift an empty bar. Lifting until "failure" didn't make us losers, it made us stronger.

I had a goal of bench pressing three hundred pounds, and my One Rep Max (1RM) was two hundred and seventy-five pounds. Every few weeks I would test my 1RM by getting warmed up and adding five pounds to the bar to see if I could lift more weight. One morning I was able to lift two hundred and eighty pounds once. I rested for a moment and added five pounds. I failed to lift two hundred and eighty-five pounds that day. This didn't mean I was a loser. The failure revealed my current limitation. I was *"failing my way to strength."*

Potentially

I grew up within a family that was obsessed with motorsports. Land, water, snow, or road, we had a toy for them all. Possessing said toy wasn't enough in our family. It wasn't enough for us to have a fast toy either; it had to be faster than yours. And we made sure of it. We were constantly working on the potential of our snowmobiles, motorcycles, boats, and cars.

I once owned a street bike capable of going zero to sixty miles per hour in less than four seconds, and zero to one hundred in ten seconds or less. It was the fastest thing I have ever owned. The motorcycle was full of potential but wouldn't move an inch without me applying the throttle. The same is true for you and me.

God's Gift

You have a gift. A gift from God. However, gifting alone is not enough. It requires attention, practice, discipline, and hard work. Sadly, our society has made "work" a four-letter word. Work is an act of worship. Worship to the Gift-giver for the gift He has given to us.

I once heard a great story that illustrates this point:

> "A certain man is out for a walk when he passes a beautiful flower garden. It was so stunning that he stopped to admire it. He noticed another man on his hands and knees working the soil. The walker says to the man working the garden, 'What a beautiful garden the Lord has made.' The gardener popped his head up above one of the plants looking for the person the voice belonged to before replying with a smile. 'You should have seen it when the Lord had it Himself.'"

I Found What I've Been Looking For

It is heartbreaking to me when I hear a presentation of the Gospel of Jesus Christ reduced to an invitation to go to a future heaven. The message of Jesus and the first century church leaders was almost entirely an invitation to a present possibility.

Don't get me wrong, I am so grateful for a future heaven, but heaven is not the prize. It's a venue. The prize is Jesus, and His promise of salvation was more than an event that you experience after your earth suit expires. Jesus said, "If you will lose your ego, you'll find your dream."

That is a promise that can be experienced right now, not just in the afterlife. Maybe you are familiar with the Bible, and you don't remember the verse being worded quite like that. The verse is found in Matthew 16:25 (NLT) and it says,

> "If you try to hang on to your life, you will lose it. But if you give up your life for my sake, you will save it."

The word "life" appears in this verse twice, and in the original text (Greek) it is the word *psyche*. A word that means "mind" and is also used to describe "ego." The invitation is to "lose your ego now and find your life — **now.**"

What Are You Waiting For?

The Apostle Paul, who contributed thirteen of the twenty-seven books in the New Testament of the Bible, wrote a great deal about living in a new reality — now. It was his prayer for the church to awaken to all that Jesus had provided for her. In his letter to the church in Ephesus, he pens this prayer.

Ephesians 1:18 (NIV) says,

> "I pray that the eyes of your heart (mind) may be enlightened in order that you may know the hope to which he has called you, the

*riches of his glorious inheritance in his holy
people."*

I want to draw attention to the word *"inheritance"* in
Paul's prayer. An inheritance isn't something you get
when you die; it is something that you get when
someone else dies.

The Apostle Paul was praying that the church would
wake up and see what Jesus had given them as an
inheritance. One that He had "called you" to live in –
now. His prayer was not a request for something more
or something new, but rather that the church would
see what they already have.

What we believe about ourselves will have a profound
impact on the way we conduct our lives, how we
behave, and how we treat others. The battle with
balance is a human struggle. We tend to overcorrect
and go from one ditch to the other. We struggle to
find the middle of the road.

There are extremes and perversions in every arena of
life. When we find ourselves in one extreme or the
other, it tends to wear us out, isolate us, and make us
selfish. The gifts and talents that you have been
generously blessed with are intended to benefit others,
not just you. Let's visit two extremes.

Certainly Not Me

One ditch is that you do nothing with the gift and
talent you have received. This is unfortunate, selfish,
and lazy. You are kidding yourself if you try and
masquerade your behavior as humility. It's false
humility and ego-centered. We have a Creator and

therefore the Creator is the one who defines the creation.

If the Creator says you are a teacher and gifts you with this talent, it is not humility to deny it or excuse it away. Someone might say, "*I could never do that, I am not good at speaking in front of people, I am not smart enough, no one in my family has ever gone to college, etc....*"

Genuine humility is agreeing with what God says about you above what you say about you.

Gifts and callings are not reduced to church ministry or what is thought of as traditional religious service. Very few people are "*called*" to this kind of work. I am a pastor because it is my calling, but it is no more important of a gift than an accountant, teacher, business owner, mechanic, or stay-at-home mom.

What's important is what we do with our talent. Leo Buscaglia puts it this way, "*Your talent is God's gift to you. What you do with it is your gift back to God.*"

I would even add that it is a gift to humanity.

Too Sexy and I Know It
The opposite extreme, the other ditch, is pride. Psychologists sometimes refer to this group as Narcissists. A narcissist is a person who has an excessive interest in or admiration of themselves.

We attempt to justify this behavior by calling it confident. Confidence is important, but pride is not rooted in confidence. Pride is rooted in insecurity. Being proud and being prideful are very different and rooted in very different soil.

And Proud of It!

Being proud is based on truth or fact. For example, I am proud to celebrate every wedding anniversary with Becky. I am proud of my oldest child, Grace, my only daughter who recently got married and started her life outside my covering. They're doing great.

Being proud of these things brings me confidence because they are rooted in truth, reality, experience, and fact. I am confident that Becky and I will celebrate decades more of marriage, and I am confident that my sons will transition well into adulthood like their older sister.

Pride causes us to be takers instead of contributors. It demands praise, acknowledgement, titles, and spotlight. Instead of using your gift and talents to help, rescue, build up, serve, or provide, you become a vacuum that sucks in everything that it can until there is nothing left to take. Therefore, many who are in this ditch are single, divorced, and have few or no long-term friendships.

As challenging as it can be to maintain, there is a middle of the road. It's best described as "managing the tension." The pull to either ditch will be a consistent battle throughout our lives, and more difficult during certain seasons. The tension exists between living as one who has nothing to offer while fighting to remain grateful for the talent that has been gifted to us.

To be poured into and have no outlet is to become like the Dead Sea – stagnant. Nothing can survive in that environment. Likewise, a river without boundaries has no direction. A river without boundaries becomes a swamp and is not attractive to others.

The benefit of collaborating with the Gift-giver is that you are fulfilled and others are blessed by you. It is like a garden hose.

The Key: Stay Connected

I have a water faucet on the side of my house. For my garden, swimming pool, and lawn to benefit from it, I need to attach a garden hose. The hose attached to the faucet distributes water wherever I need it. If the hose is attached to the water faucet, the hose remains full. So full that it overflows. If I detach the hose from the faucet, eventually the hose empties out and has nothing to dispense.

The very same is true for you and me. When we collaborate with God (our source), our lives are full. In fact, we have surplus and can distribute blessings to others. The moment ego takes over and we detach from our Source, we begin to dry up. Nothing flowing into us, and nothing flowing out of us. Ditch your ego. Stay connected. Be a blessing.

CHAPTER 8

Responsibility

It's time to put the victim to bed
and awake the hero instead.

Responsibility

*"Blame is projecting our responsibility rather than
acknowledging that responsibility starts with you."*
— Danny Silk

Cut It Out

Nothing brings your dreams to a halt faster than when
you blame. The moment you blame, you forfeit power
and become a victim.

Over time we adopt the mind-set, and a victim
mentality becomes our operating system. In some
cases, we have been truly victimized, and I am in no
way attempting to minimize the trauma. Additionally,
if you are currently being abused, you need to seek
help.

The point that I intend to make is that <u>you are NOT powerless</u>. Taking responsibility begins with a decision. A determination that you will no longer be controlled by your past, a wound, a disappointment, a failure, or a betrayal.

You are the gatekeeper, and you alone have the authority to control what you meditate on. The word "decision" is rooted in Latin, and literally means "*to cut off.*" Deciding is about cutting off choices – cutting you off from some other course of action. To move forward we are going to have to divorce the story we continue to play in our minds.

If we change our minds, we will change our lives. It is as simple as changing where you look, where you focus. When we do, we'll stop tripping over what is behind us. You don't have to like it to accept it, but you must accept it to move forward.

Purpose in the Pain

A perfect example is Wesley Chapman, founder of A HUMAN PROJECT. Chapman and his siblings suffered torture, neglect, and sexual abuse from their step-father. Wesley is the oldest of his siblings and blamed himself for being powerless to rescue them from the abuse.

He was only six and a half years old when his mother abandoned him because of his incessant crying, breakdowns, and fits as a result of the abuse. The final encounter with his mom and step-dad involved him being hung upside down on a clothesline in the backyard. His step-dad held a knife to his neck and swore to kill him and everyone he loved if he ever told anyone about the abuse again. And he didn't. At least not until adulthood. He struggled with guilt, shame, and debilitating depression. Wesley even attempted to end his own life several times.

It all changed when he had a powerful revelation that there was purpose in the pain. Chapman declared, "It is time to put the victim to bed and awake the hero instead."

At the age of thirty, Wesley Chapman left his seven-figure business behind and set out on a journey that would lead him to saving the lives of thousands of children around the world. He founded A HUMAN PROJECT, a for-purpose 501c3, with a mission to create a community of empowered youth.

Today, through A HUMAN PROJECT, Chapman brings hope, understanding, options, and empowerment to act. So many children live in dysfunction caused by abuse, neglect, abandonment, and drugs. This leads to low self-esteem, suicide, bullying, and a cycle of unhappiness. Wes is on a mission to help 25 million people rise above trials as they discover their own life purposes. He believes that every child is created for a purpose and that each child deserves to experience ultimate joy. To find purpose in the pain.

There is an unfair assumption that successful people must not have had the same challenges as you. They must have had it easier, received a big break, grew up on the right-side of the tracks, or been born with more talent than the rest of us. Sure, there are some that would fall under one or more of those examples, but most successful people have had to overcome challenges that you know nothing about.

Nobody Has It Easy

Oprah Winfrey, for example, was just nine years old when she began suffering sexual abuse by her then nineteen-year-old cousin. She was also severely beaten and molested by other relatives. She turned to substances in order to cope with her struggles. At fourteen, she was sent to live with her father and discovered she was pregnant. Sadly, the baby – a boy – was born two months premature and passed away at just two weeks old. Today, Winfrey is a billionaire media giant and philanthropist. Oprah Winfrey is best known for hosting her own internationally popular talk show from 1986 to 2011. From there, she launched her own television network, OWN.

Tyler Perry, a successful actor and producer, had a very tragic youth. He suffered sexual and physical abuse from his family and a neighbor. On one occasion, while his mother was out, his father came home "drunk" and "mad at the world" and got the vacuum cleaner extension cord. He trapped him in a room and beat him with it until the skin was coming off his back. Today he is a writer, actor, producer, and director. Tyler Perry has built an entertainment empire that consists of successful films, plays, and a best-selling book.

Abraham Lincoln, who is regarded as one of the best U.S. Presidents, had to overcome nearly thirty years of challenges which included multiple business failures, tragic losses, defeats, and a mental breakdown prior to winning the White House. Lincoln's advice, *"Always bear in mind that your own resolution to succeed is more important than any other one thing."*

Steve Jobs, co-founder of Apple, started life with his blue-collar adoptive family in San Francisco. Jobs's adoptive father was a "repo-man," and his adoptive mother was a stay-at-home mom. Jobs once said, *"I'm convinced that about half of what separates the successful entrepreneurs from the non-successful ones is pure perseverance."*

Jobs understood the path to success is a roller coaster. There are ups, and there are downs. There are the highest of highs and the lowest of lows. Persistence is vital. As Jim Rohn said, *"If you really want to do something, you'll find a way. If you don't, you'll find an excuse."*

The sinister thing about excuses is that they're valid. The decision is yours whether to allow them to endorse your situation or use them to encourage you to press on.

Busy, Busy

When we take responsibility, we take our life back. In most cases it won't be some magical one-time event where everything is suddenly cleaned up. It's going to be more like cleaning a dirty room.

Something that gets put off because it feels overwhelming and is difficult to get excited about because we don't notice the change right away. You have a list of excuses why the room ended up this way, and if it were not for _____ (you fill in the blank), it wouldn't have gotten this messy.

Maybe so, but it is still your room, and no one else is going to clean it for you. The same is true in our lives.

We have dozens of excuses why our lives are in disorder, but our favorite go-to is "we're busy."

Think about how you respond to the question, *"How have you been?"*

It is usually *"I've been busy."*

Busy is a broad term and difficult to quantify. I made a conscious decision a couple of years ago to stop using this response. After all, when is the last time we weren't busy?

It had become a knee-jerk response that made me feel important or needed. Even if *"busy"* meant busy about nothing – the person asking didn't know the difference. Busy becomes a cop out, a justification, an excuse as to why your life isn't where you want it to be. It easily leads to blame. We blame the boss, the workload, the season, our spouse, and our kids. Instead of taking responsibility, we postpone.

We begin saying things like, "When things slow down I will get to it." As life does, it runs in cycles, and you get a window of opportunity when things – slow down. And you would do it, but first a break. After all, you've been busy, and you deserve a break.

1440

What is busy exactly? According to Merriam-Webster dictionary, busy is defined as *"full of activity."*

So that begs an even better question. Does all activity possess equal benefit? Of course not.

What if most of the activity that is wearing us out is not benefiting our lives, families, goals, and dreams? What if we acknowledged that each one of us is given the same fourteen hundred and forty minutes each day? Each of us will consume, spend, and lose this time. Gone. Forever.

Time doesn't stop for anyone. You cannot buy, slow, or speed up time. The only way to make time your friend is to manage it.

You alone are the manager of your life, and that means you must take responsibility for how your time is spent, invested, and converted.

Moving On

My encouragement is to review your daily activities and write down what it is that keeps you so busy. This will require you to be honest with yourself. As difficult as it may be to admit, write down the accurate amount of time you spend doing each activity.

The purpose of this task is not meant to discourage or cause self-loathing or shame. It is simply an assessment to determine a starting point. When you review your past, come up with an interpretation that empowers you.

Think in terms of *"That is where I used to be. I am not there now. I am growing. Today is a new day and a new opportunity to reclaim my life. I am taking responsibility!"*

Ain't No Shame in My Game

This is vitally important because shame will attempt to do the opposite of taking responsibility. Shame doesn't just acknowledge an event, failure, mistake, or pattern. No, shame will tell you *"that is who you are."*

In order to break the power of shame, you need to respond to the accusing thoughts with, *"That is what I did, but it is not who I am!"*

Identity is the most powerful tool in assigning value to yourself. What we believe about ourselves will determine what activities are valuable. It will govern what we allow and what needs to be added, reduced, or removed.

In addition to empowering us to take charge of our schedule, identity also empowers us to combat criticism. The presence of a critic is a sign of progress. The biggest opportunities come with the greatest resistance. When we're running with the pack, we blend in with the masses.

The moment we adjust our personal standards and take a step toward our purpose, we separate from the crowd. This will reveal the insecurity of some and threaten their ego. You don't have to say a word, point a finger, or give an opinion about what they are or are not doing. The decision was personal. The standard was yours and imposed on you alone, but insecurity hears, *"I am better than you."*

Our aim in pursuing our purpose is not to show others up, but to show others what is possible.

There's Got to Be More Than This!

The courage to pursue something bigger than you, to become more than you are, and risk others seeing you make mistakes along the way is hard. If it were easy, everyone would do it.

There is a desire in the depths of our souls that cries out, *"I am created for more than this."*

When we suppress that voice with excuses, it makes us angry people, and anger never gets buried alive. It usually comes out when we see people doing what we wish we had the courage to do ourselves. Critics are like billboards, not stop signs. You're going to pass dozens of them on your way to your destination.

"You'll Never..."

I have discovered each time I have been told "you'll never _____," I end up excelling at it. Some critics form their opinion of what you can accomplish based on what they believe about themselves. If "they" can't do it, then certainly "you" can't either.

Other critics formulate their opinion based on others who have tried and failed, or they perceive it to be too much of a longshot.

History shows that God loves to use ordinary people to do extraordinary things. He is King of the longshot. Deciding to follow God's lead over the voice of the critics is the key to defying the odds.

Faith is our confident response to what God says is possible, and God will never invite you to a life where He is not necessary. Jesus boldly said, "Apart from me you can do nothing."

I like to reverse engineer this scripture and say, "With Jesus I can do anything."

To experience an extraordinary life, you are going to have to do "extra."

The question shouldn't be "Am I ready?" The question you need to ask yourself is, "Am I willing?"

Are You Willing?

The summer of 2011 was one of the biggest *"Am I willing?"* moments for me and my family. I had been promoted to a newly created position, the position that I had been working toward for my entire career. I received a sizable pay increase, bonus incentives, and additional stock options. I was traveling both nationally and internationally as part of a dynamic team on the frontlines of innovation and progress.

I had always been involved in church ministry and had served as a bi-vocational minister after being licensed in 2001. My wife and I have served in many different roles in different churches in different states. I had never received compensation for doing ministry and had always served on a volunteer basis, and I was glad to do so. Afterall, God was blessing me with increase and opportunity in the marketplace.

In June of 2011, Becky and I started a Bible study in the home of our closest friends. Something we felt God had prompted us to do. The location of our friend's house was literally in the middle of nowhere. After traveling thirty minutes away from the city, you would exit the interstate and travel a two-lane highway for many miles before turning onto a rural dirt road. Then there was two miles of dirt road before turning onto a driveway more than a quarter mile long. The drive disappeared into a section woods to a secluded hideaway.

This was anything but convenient, and not what *"church planters"* say is best practice. No worries, I wasn't a church planter.

I was amazed at how many people came that first evening, and how many routinely came that summer. We were having a great time.

What started as a Bible study was about to lead to, *"Are you willing to start a church?"*

Waiting on You.

When I finally mustered the courage to approach the topic with our core group, I said, *"I feel like God wants me to start a church. If I did, would any of you join me?"*

Our core group consisted of eight adults. They all responded with *"We've been waiting for you to say it."*

And so, we did. On October 1, 2011 we established a non-profit 501c3 and were officially a ministry. Barely two weeks later we became aware of a church that had closed, and the building was available. With less than seven hundred dollars in a church bank account, barely two weeks old on paper, and a series of miraculous events, we closed on our first building on November 6, 2011.

The church building was in the small village of Eagle, Michigan. Population one hundred and nine. The team and I went to work to prepare the space for an official launch in January of 2012.

The church began to steadily grow, and by the time we reached August 2012, a decision had to be made. I could no longer keep pace with the demands of the ministry and manage the engineering group. To leave my job was to leave certainty, benefits, bonuses, stock options, 401K, and my dream position. Becky and I knew that this was the next step God had for us, and I planned my exit strategy with the company.

Enter Critics

My grandfather was so angry with my "foolish" decision that he changed his estate plan. I had proven to him that I could not be trusted to make good decisions, and therefore could not be entrusted to see after his financial affairs should he pass away. My grandfather spent the final five years of his life disgusted with me and consumed with the expectation that I would fail and would expect him to bail me out.

My hero died never being proud of me. And he made sure that I knew it. I had other family members and close friends who scolded me for being irresponsible. *"You have a family to support,"* they would say, and they would usually follow up with a litany of interrogating questions with worst case scenarios.

"You Know ..."

One Sunday morning we had a couple visit the church. After the service, the husband approached me for what I thought was an introduction.

"You know," he began as he looked around the room. Continuing after a brief pause, he said, *"They say you should never start a church in a building that looks like a church."*

To which I replied with a facial expression and head nod that implied *"You don't say!"*

But he wasn't done. And as if the thought shot into his mind by surprise, he blurted out, *"Oh, and they say you should never start a church outside of a metropolitan area either."*

So, with a touch of dramatic sarcasm, I looked over his right shoulder and then his left. I turned my head slightly over my right shoulder, looking behind me. Then I looked him in the eyes and said, *"I didn't pick the building. Jesus did. And I didn't pick the location either. That was Jesus, too. And as you can see by the crowd, He seems to know more than 'they' do."*

He and his wife did visit again. What I have noticed about critics, especially the most vocal ones, is that they have never built anything themselves. Successful people are too busy building their own businesses, ministries, and dreams to criticize yours.

Wrong Direction

Have you found yourself going the wrong direction and being embarrassed about it? You've run through the scenarios in your mind of what people will say or think. Each time your imagination plays out something worse.

Here is what I have observed. Most people are so consumed with their own issues, they hardly notice anyone else's. Of course, there are always a few who are looking for a juicy story to share around the watercooler. For them to feed their gossip addiction, they are always hunting for another story to share. Your story will lose their interest the moment they gather intel on someone else.

U-turn

Consider this: have you ever been on a road and taken a wrong turn or exit? I have. Usually I catch it quickly, but there have been a couple of times that I was a solid half an hour down the road going in the wrong the direction.

What did I do? If I followed the model that many live their lives by, I would just keep going. I had a destination in mind, but I guess it wasn't meant to be. I'll just keep going and see where this route takes me.

No way! The very second I discovered I was heading the wrong way, I was looking for a turnaround or exit.

Was I aggravated? Of course! Embarrassed? For a minute. Did it cost me time? Yes, and that may have been the bigger irritation for me, but I wasn't going to abandon the purpose of my trip because I was delayed.

And you shouldn't forfeit your destiny because you made a wrong turn.

Redeemed

The moment you take responsibly and turn around, you are immediately redeeming your time. The word "deem" means to own. When you "redeem" time, it means you are reclaiming ownership again. You're paying yourself back for the time you lost, and when your debt is repaid, you are gaining ground again.

The sooner you turn around, the less amount of time needs to be repaid. Drop your ego and redeem your time.

CHAPTER 9

Start Small and Believe Big

"If you plan to excel in big things, you have to develop the habit in the small ones." – LeCrae

It Takes Time

I would rank myself among the people who struggle with patience. I don't like the *"long way"* to anything. I choose the interstate over side roads, and I struggle to maintain posted speed limits. I am a big fan of take-out as opposed to dining-in, and I choose flying over driving every time.

I draw the line when it comes to microwave ovens, however. It's true that I use a microwave every day for various warm ups, but when it comes to cooking, there is no match for slow-cooked food. With microwaves you usually get one of two outcomes. The food item is lava hot on the outside with ice crystals on the inside, or the food only remains hot for a few minutes. Usually just long enough to scald your mouth.

The best things in life take time. I don't want my dream to be half cooked or lose intensity before its time. If you are like me, you are driven. You want to push forward, build, and accomplish. Keep in mind that everything starts small. An oak tree is in the seed, a skyscraper begins with one brick, and Disney World started as a mouse.

I have observed two extremes in human behavior. On one side we have a group of people who want the keys to the kingdom, and they want them right now! The other extreme is a group that suffers from "analysis paralysis" and fears engagement.

Convincing either group to begin is a challenge. The first group can appear to feel entitled, but I think it has more to do with naivety.

It doesn't help that we have a culture that celebrates and even rewards people for going "viral." A perfect example of this is Danielle Bregoli.

"Cash Me Outside, How 'bout Dat"

In 2016, when she was thirteen, Bregoli first appeared on the Dr. Phil show to be interviewed about stealing her mother's car. The young lady spoke so unintelligibly that Dr. Phil asked, "Do you have an accent?"

Her mother acted as a translator and sheepishly told Dr. Phil that her accent came from the "street." Her grammar was so poor that Dr. Phil asked if she had finished the fifth grade. During her sit down on a segment called, "I Want to Give Up My Car-Stealing, Knife-Wielding, Twerking 13-Year-Old Daughter Who Tried To Frame Me For a Crime," Bregoli used the catchphrase "*cash me outside, how 'bout dat*" to insinuate that she would fight any of the women in the studio audience that day.

The video of the episode has been viewed more than fifty million times on YouTube. The memes and video clips that flooded the internet were meanspirited and degrading, yet it launched Bregoli into stardom. She is now an internet personality, travels the world as a female rap artist, and is worth several millions of dollars.

Trendy

Scenarios like this and other sad examples have many young people thinking that this is the way to fame and fortune. The art of building something or becoming someone has been traded for building a following on a social media platform and hoping for your viral moment. Even if it costs you your self-respect.

The so-called connected world has also made its mark on the group that is afraid to commit. The influence of popular opinion or "*likes*" on your social media has paralyzed people from making decisions. Instead of zealously discovering their God-given gift and pursuing their passion, they have been programed to do what is "*trending*" online. The problem with trends is that they change. Daily.

Have you ever met someone who you really admired or who is famous, only to discover that they are not the same person they portray in the limelight? I have.

But I have also met some quality men and woman who are even better in person than I had imagined.

The term *"quality"* can mean a lot of things to different people, so for the sake of making a specific point, I want to hone in on one characteristic that really impresses me.

That Don't Impress Me Much

It is easy to be impressed by someone's accomplishments, innovations, earnings, and fame. It is, however, very unattractive when the individual is so impressed with themselves that they feel entitled. They are so filled with ego that they are unwilling to share their story. After all, they've *"arrived,"* and if you want their kind of success, you'll have to figure it out on your own.

Instead of remembering how ugly it looked or how poorly it made them feel when someone looked down on them when they were still working the grind, they take the opportunity to do the same. It is as if it's their rite of passage. Thankfully, not every successful person is like that.

A Story to Tell

There are people who start with a vision and dedicate themselves to their dream. With hard work and God's grace, they have become successful. Influential even. Whether they built an empire, amassed great wealth, or created life-changing innovation, they remained unpretentious. They didn't start reading and believing their own headlines.

They have a story that begins with nothing but hope and possibility. A narrative that includes missteps,

120

failures, and betrayals. They experienced challenges that if they didn't talk about, you would never know of them. But in my mind that is what makes them such a quality person. They want to share their story. A story that includes the good and the bad so that it might benefit other aspiring entrepreneurs, innovators, ministry leaders, and dreamers.

There is an old Chinese proverb that says, "*The best time to plant a tree was 20 years ago. The second-best time is now.*"

We get into trouble when we look at someone else's twenty-year-old tree and compare it to the seed in our hand. Everything that is needed to become a tall, mighty oak is in the seed.

There are no short cuts. What we do with the seed will determine our future. If we desire to have a similar outcome as another successful person, we should follow a similar path that they did.

How do we know what that path is? We ask. Ditch your ego and seek their wisdom.

"*I don't have access to people like this,*" you may be thinking.

Yes, you do! Thanks to the internet we can order books or their biographies. You can listen to TED Talks and podcasts. Another forgotten treasure is the local library. You can borrow books, audio books, and use the internet for free. There is no shortage of information and ways that we can access incredible examples of small beginnings.

I don't know about you, but I would much rather learn from someone else's mistakes than to experience them firsthand. Success leaves clues and learning principles. Applied by successful people they may save us years or even decades.

I Want Some of That

There is a difference between envy and jealousy, and ego will determine which one will show up in your life and mine. Envy is a desire to have a quality, possession, or other desirable attribute belonging to someone else. There are people that I admire and esteem highly. There may be qualities or attributes that I recognize as something that I desire to have as well.

This pushes me to aim higher and encourages me to know that if it is possible for them, it is possible for me, too. Jealousy is altogether another thing. It's a monster birthed form ego.

Jealousy is recognizing that another person possesses something that you do not, and it makes you angry. A jealous person is not happy until the other person no longer has it either. Jealousy will cause you to divert your energy from working your own field to attempting to chop down the other person's tree. Ugly.

Short Cut or Short Lived?

There will always be a temptation to skip the process, jump ahead, and shave time. Sometimes you can get away with it, but the risk is high.

About twenty-five years ago my step-father decided to dig a pond on his property. What began as a small pet project quickly grew into a full-blown excavation development. After a couple of years of renting larger and larger excavators and running bulldozers to grade the property around the now small lake, it was done.

But it was barren. The property was in desperate need of trees and landscaping. The idea of waiting decades for trees to grow was daunting, so he contacted a local tree farm and had some mature trees delivered and planted.

They looked nice, but it needed more. In an attempt to save money and time, my step-dad decided he would locate and transplant some trees from another area of his property to the pond. How difficult could it be? He was no arborist, but clearly he could dig.

What he didn't know (because he didn't ask) is that digging a tree for transplanting can remove as much as ninety percent of the absorbing roots which causes transplant shock to the tree. If the tree has poor health, the rates of survival and recovery will be low. And only a couple of the transplanted trees survived.

Everything Looked Fine
There is a lot to be learned from the process, and bypassing steps doesn't always show up right away. It can be years down the road before the problem manifests. It may look good from a distance or from the outside, but the fruit will give it away.

A friend of mine tells a great story that illustrates this point perfectly. Near the college he attended was a large grapefruit orchard. The orchard would hire ambitious college kids and pay them by the bushel.

He would utilize the orchard for date money. He learned that the faster he could pick, the quicker he earned his fun money. He discovered that the fastest way to pick grapefruits was to climb mid-way up the tree and shake it for all it was worth. The grapefruits would fall to the ground, and he would gather bushels in a snap.

One Friday afternoon, in a hurry to earn some date money, he jumped into a tree as he had done dozens of times before. But on this occasion, as soon as he shook the tree, it split in half. My friend fell to the ground. He was in shock and then instantly grew worried that he was going to be in some trouble.

One of the property managers saw what happened and came to make sure he wasn't hurt. The manager noticed my friend's concerned expression and reassured him that it wasn't his fault. The tree was sick.

"How do you know?" my friend asked.

The man pointed to the center of the tree which was decaying from the inside. He then reached down and grabbed a grapefruit. On the outside the fruit looked as good as all the other trees. That is until the man cut the grapefruit in half and revealed that the fruit was rotten.

It's a Process

It is true that some successful people were provided a jump start which gave them an advantage, but it is the minority. According to a 2017 survey conducted by Spectrem Group, the U.S. now has close to 11 million millionaires. Dr. Tom Stanley, author of *The Millionaire Next Door*, found through his research that about twenty percent of millionaires became that way through inheritance. The other eighty percent are first-generation millionaires.

It is not that having a net worth of a million dollars is the final indicator that you are successful, but success is something that is more commonly achieved by process rather than inheritance.

Ten Steps to Success

If you want to teach a child how to count to one hundred, all you need to do is teach them to count to ten. Once they know how to count to ten, they just start over again at eleven. The process of counting to ten repeatedly will get them to one hundred.

Starting small and believing big is much like counting to one hundred; you must start at one. Let's call "Level One" counting to ten. As you grow in knowledge, competency, and experience, you get promoted.

Eventually you reach number ten, which is the highest proficiency at "Level One." You have become the best. You are the go-to person at this level. Because of your acquired skillset, in time you are offered another promotion. And this time you move up to "Level Two."

At level two you are offered a higher degree of responsibility, influence, and income. But you must be willing to begin at one again. For you to excel at a new level, you must be willing to start small and believe big. Ditch your ego and continue to grow.

You're reading this book because you have desires, dreams, and ambitions. Me too! I get you. Perhaps like me you have read many of the classic personal growth and self-help books. Books that include: *The Richest Man in Babylon* by George Clason, *How to Win Friends and Influence People* by Dale Carnegie, *Think and Grow Rich* by Napoleon Hill, *Rich Dad Poor Dad* by Robert Kiyosaki, and *Good to Great* by Jim

Collins to name a few. All these books have had measurable influence on me, yet all the wisdom in these books can be found in the book of Proverbs. One of my favorite proverbs, written by King Solomon, is found in Proverbs 13:18 (ESV). He writes,

> "Poverty and disgrace come to him who ignores instruction, but whoever heeds reproof is honored."

Teachable

The word *honored* in this verse means to be *"glorified"* or *"exalted."* The timeless truth that I believe can be extracted from this verse is that while we continue to believe big, we must stay small in our mind.

I am not talking about a defeatist mindset or small expectations but to rather remain teachable. You may have been the big fish in the small pond, but when you get promoted, you become a small fish again.

What you learned from the previous level has prepared you for the next, but there is much to learn. I have heard it said, *"There is a reason why God created us with two ears and only one mouth. It is because we need to listen twice as much as we talk!"*

Value-Add

You were promoted because of the value you bring to the team, the organization, or the market. There is a way that you can offer your insight and remain teachable. I found that this simple approach greatly benefitted me and the organizations that I worked for. I also appreciate this approach when members of my staff and team follow this model.

CEOs, Presidents, Vice Presidents, Division Managers, and Supervisors all have big picture vision. They don't know the small, precise, or trivial details like you may. It is also likely that they do not possess the specific skill set and training that you have. They are counting on your expertise to advise them.

If you think you are being a good soldier by being a "yes" man/woman, then you need to tune in here. If you have information, expertise, or perspective that your boss does not have, you are not serving the organization by keeping quiet.

Allow me to provide you with a fictitious and exaggerated situation that will make this point. Let's say the company you work for is having an issue with wind gusts blowing the exterior doors open. When this happens, it blows product all over the manufacturing area. In this scenario, you are a tradesman, and your boss asked you to go through the facility and weld all the steel doors closed. It is true that welding all the steel doors closed would keep the doors from blowing open, but you know that it creates a host of other problems. You could be a "yes" man, take your marching orders, and go out and weld all the doors closed. Or you could respond to your boss by saying, *"I will do it because you are my supervisor, but based on what I know, I recommend that we do it this way instead. And this is why ...."*

It has been my experience that structuring a response like this is received with genuine appreciation. It provides honor to the supervisor and provides a safe way for them to change their initial request without having their authority called into question. Your supervisor may know something that you do not and stick to their original request. Either way, you have established yourself as a valued team member who brings their attention to details that are important to making good decisions.

CHAPTER 10

Promotion Please!

NO • EGO

People will follow you,
pay you, and promote you
based on results.

Promotion

*"You don't get promoted based on what you **can** become, you get promoted because of what you **have** become."* – Phillip McKinney

Changing Places

As mentioned in the previous chapter, there are steps within each level of responsibility. Like counting to ten, ten being the top tier of your current level, we grow more proficient in our role. With time, experience, and proven determination, we master the level.

According to the Merriam-Webster Dictionary, the word promotion means, *"The act or fact of being raised in position or rank."*

Promotion is made up of two words, the prefix "pro" and the word "motion." The prefix *pro* means *"forward,"* and the word *motion* means *"an act of changing places."* In other words, it is the next logical step.

The home I currently live in has a second floor. My children's bedrooms are located on the second floor, and as such they are making their way up and down the staircase routinely. It would be unreasonable for me to expect that they could travel from the first floor to the second floor in one single step. In fact, it would be impossible even for the most athletic of individuals.

However, with the dozen or so steps between floors, the task of going to the next level is very systematic. One step at a time. Each step is one step closer to an elevated space, a promotion.

Becoming

An additional aspect that is vitally important to understand about promotion is the process of *"becoming."*

You may possess knowledge, but that does not translate into ability. I, for example, know the mechanics of a bench press exercise. Knowing how to bench press four hundred pounds and having the ability are two very different things.

This is perhaps the most crushing aspect of premature promotion. The effects can be as devastating on the organization as the individual. I wholeheartedly believe that I can gain the strength needed to perform a one repetition max (1RM) of four hundred pounds. The key word being *gain*.

The Apostle Paul warned his understudy Timothy about promoting an individual into leadership too early. He used the term *novice* to describe someone who was not yet proven in smaller tasks before leading an organization.

I speak with many people who are praying for increase, blessing, and promotion. After spending some time discussing in more detail what they are asking for, I often find myself telling them, *"It would be cruel of the Lord to answer that prayer."*

Usually it is met with a surprised expression and requires further explanation. If the Lord provided what they were asking for right now, it would be like me sliding under a barbell platted with four-hundred pounds. It would crush me, and their request would crush them.

The process of "becoming" is the blessing of God. With every step, at every level, we gain the strength needed to manage more.

Not for a Novice

The process of *becoming* will weed out those who want promotion for the wrong reasons. Many seek titles and places of authority because of insecurity. If you have ever worked for an insecure boss, you know how miserable it is.

Picking back up on the Apostle Paul's warning to Timothy about promoting *novices*, he provides good reason. 1 Timothy 3:6-7 (TPT) says,

> "He should not be a new disciple who would be vulnerable to living in the clouds of conceit and fall into pride, making him

> *easy prey for Satan. He should be respected by those who are unbelievers, having a beautiful testimony among them so that he will not fall into the traps of Satan and be disgraced."*

Lack of experience lends to arrogance, or as Paul says, conceit. I remember when I was in my late teens and early twenties. I knew everything! You didn't even have to ask my opinion about a subject, I was interjecting with my profound wisdom whenever possible. I was so sure that other people's challenges and obstacles would never be an issue for me.

Experience has shown me different, and I have had to apologize to several individuals for my early arrogance. The second warning in this passage of scripture is a lack of established respect and evidence (testimony) of consistency. Trust is earned and requires time and testing. We must be willing to establish a good reputation. One consistent act at a time.

Whether or not people let on that you are being watched, you are. Do you arrive on time or early? Do you keep deadlines? Are you productive, and do you go extra-mile? Keep in mind that reputation is what others think about you, and their opinion is built on performance, not intention.

Results

Discipline establishes trust, and people will trust you because of your results. Postponing the urgency to establish disciplines in your life will only delay your success. It's ego that says, "You promote me first, and I'll show you what I can do."

NO EGO

If you really believe that statement, I dare you then to give your car keys to your ten-year-old. Give them the opportunity to *"show you what they can do"* with your $35,000 vehicle. You and I both know that isn't going to happen. Neither is your promotion without proven results.

The subject of discipline is going to be the topic of any self-help or personal growth book you read. I don't want to insult your intelligence by stating the obvious, *"You need discipline."*

Instead, I want to encourage you with a principle that will help you with discipline in your life. It's hard! If it were easy, we'd all have amazing physiques, overflowing savings accounts, and retirement portfolios that would allow us to retire early. It is not a matter of knowing what to do; it is the ability to put into action what we know.

The key I want to share with you is equivalent to fuel in your car's gas tank. One word: vision.

Vision
The wisdom of King Solomon was so impressive that people in his day would travel from all over the known world to meet with him, to observe what he had accomplished, and to seek his other worldly wisdom.

He revealed that vision is the source of discipline. Solomon writes Proverbs 29:18 (NASB),

> *"Where there is no vision, the people are unrestrained, but happy is he who keeps the law."*

Did you catch that? The absence of vision leads to an undisciplined life. Conversely, having a vision is the source (fuel) of discipline.

What is vision? Vision is the address you intend to go to. It's your destination. When I am driving to a place that I have never been, I type the address into my phone, and it will provide me with the most direct route.

Having a vision simplifies your life. People with a vision are less stressed. Stress comes from not knowing what to do. Having a vision will control your life.

Once you know where you want to go, you won't waste your time taking unnecessary detours. A vision will define you. It will determine what you say "yes" or "no" to.

I'm Going Somewhere

A vision for your dream and for your life will keep you focused. America's #1 Confidence Coach, Dr. Keith Johnson, says it best. *"Where focus goes, energy flows, and results show."*

A river is a great example of this. A river without boundaries is a swamp, and swamps are stinky and unattractive. Boundaries narrow the focus, direct the flow, and provide a determined destination.

If you want better results, look no further than where you spend your time. You are the product of how you spend your time.

The Key to Happiness

Happiness is tied to vision as well. Look again with me at King Solomon's wisdom. He said, *"Happy is he who keeps the law."* Proverbs 29:18 (NASB). The word *law* could be replaced with the words *"principles"* or *"keys."*

Sometimes when we hear or read the word *law*, we think of judicial ordinances, but that is not what Solomon is speaking of in this verse. Solomon is using the term law in this way: The Law of Gravity or The Law of Motion.

When we cooperate with these laws, things will go well for us. If we violate the law of gravity, for example, we will suffer the consequences, the punishment, the judgment. This makes success and failure predictable.

Success makes me *"happy!"* – how about you? Success is measured in results, and when you are disciplined, you get results. People will follow you, pay you, and promote you based on results.

Character Will Keep You There

Character is also something that is tested over time. Your competency may get you a promotion, but your character will keep you there. With every promotion there is increased authority, access to sensitive information, decision making, and someone else's money.

Weak character is easily corrupted, and we've all read the headlines of individuals who have been fired, arrested, and lost everything that they've worked for because they didn't develop their character along the way. There will be times that you will be asked or expected to compromise in order to benefit yourself or the organization. Don't fall for it.

It was a late Friday afternoon. It had already been a very long week when we received a call from one of our vendors in Toronto, Canada. It was bad news. Their primary filling and packaging machine was broken down. To experience a machine malfunction in a manufacturing environment is not that uncommon. The uniqueness of our industry was that our product was used to test for hazardous microorganisms in food. Public food safety is a big deal. If we couldn't provide the product, it wasn't like our customer could just wait for us to ship it. The customer would be forced to find alternate sources to purchase from. Most likely, one of our competitors. We could potentially lose a multi-million-dollar account.

Our ability to deliver one hundred percent of the time was such a concern for our largest international customers that we would sign a contract guaranteeing that we would never backorder or delay on shipping. This was a major issue!

To make matters worse, the facility in Toronto did not have a skilled technician to troubleshoot and repair the machine. Since it was a Friday afternoon, the odds of locating a contractor before the weekend were slim.

That's when my phone rang. I could hear the urgency in his tone and volume coming from the receiver before it reached my ear. *"I need you in my office now!"* he said and then hung up.

I promptly made my way to his office and joined the crowded room full of manic Account Executives,

Purchasing Agents, Production Schedulers, and two Vice Presidents. Conversation stopped the moment I poked my head into the door. *"I need you to pack a bag and get to Toronto by tonight,"* is all he said as the rest of the room looked at me as if to say, *"What are you still doing here?"*

"Um ... what?" I replied.

After being downloaded with the current emergency, I headed home to pack a bag and hit the road for Toronto, about a five hour drive away from our facility.

Doin Some Work, Eh?

I reached the international border at Port Huron around nine o'clock that evening. The process of crossing the border took time. The vehicle ahead of me was being inspected, and the car in the lane next to me was being circled by a border agent and his dog.

When I finally got up to the station manned by an officer, I was greeted with an open hand and a less than enthusiastic, *"Passport."*

He didn't even look up at me. At the same time, another border agent was circling my vehicle with a mirror on a stick looking under my SUV. Upon receiving my passport, he held it up between us, looking back and forth at the picture and me. *"What brings you to Canada tonight, Mr. ... ah ... McKinney?"*

By now the agent circling my vehicle had opened the rear passenger door of my vehicle and noticed the tool bag on the floor. *"I am visiting one of our vendors to* check out a production machine," I said, kind of distracted by the guy rooting around my backseat.

The officer looked at me as if I had said something wrong before responding, "What do you mean by 'check out'?"

"The machine malfunctioned today, and I am going to troubleshoot the problem," I said.

With eyebrows raised and an expression that indicated he and I were now on the same page, he said, "I see … so I will need your paperwork then."

Now it was my time to look lost. "What paperwork are you speaking of?" I asked, puzzled.

"Your pre-approved documentation with the Canadian Human Services that allows you to render services in our country," he informed me.

"I don't have that, sir," I said, realizing this was not going as planned.

"Go ahead and pull forward. Park your vehicle in front of that building," he said, pointing to the parking lot. "We'll see you inside," he said as the gate raised. I pulled ahead.

I was frustrated by the delay but had no other choice but to follow his instructions. I made my way to the parking lot just a couple of hundred feet ahead. I went inside the brick building expecting to fill out paperwork and be on my way. Behind a chest-high desk, two officers looked at me with expectant eyes.

"Passport," is all one said. After barely enough time to have been able to read my name, he said, "Mr.

McKinney, go ahead and have a seat in there." He pointed to the only open door.

I walked in the all-white room with a single stainless-steel table in the middle. It was like I entered the set of every cop show I have ever seen. The only thing missing was the cheaply dressed detective attempting to interrogate me.

After what seemed like forever, the officer appeared in the doorway and said, *"Mr. McKinney, you can come with me."* Then he immediately turned and walked away.

Good Bye

By the time I exited the door, the officer was just getting back behind the chest-high desk again. As soon as I approached the desk, the officer handed me my passport and said, *"Mr. McKinney, we've decided to let you go back home today."*

Leaning forward with a perplexed look, I hesitated. But then I managed to ask, *"Back home? You mean you were considering holding me here?"*

The officer, as stoic as before, simply responded, *"That's right. You don't have the correct paperwork to provide services in Canada."*

He noticed that I was going to ask additional questions and cut me off by pointing to the door and saying, *"Drive safe."*

And with that, I was on my way back home. I was tired, irritated, and about to make a dreaded call to my boss.

I waited until I had crossed the border and was back in the U.S. to make the call. By now it was past ten o'clock. The phone only rang once before he answered as if he was waiting for my call. *"You can't possibly be there already?"* he said instead of saying *'hello.'"*

I took a noticeably deep breath before saying, *"No. Actually I am on my way home. They turned me away at the border."*

His frustration was instant, and his language reflected it. I will translate with a family-friendly filter – *"Are you kidding me! What did you say to them?"*

"The truth!" I shot back. *"I told them that I was coming to troubleshoot a machine for our company and hoped to repair the problem. They notified me that I did not have the correct paper to execute services in Canada, and they sent me back. They considered detaining me!"*

A Lie or a Liar?
There was a long pause that I was hoping would mean that he was empathizing with me about nearly being detained. Not so much. *"Why didn't you just lie? You could have told them you were going to visit your aunt."*

There was silence. I was waiting to hear more, but he was waiting for a response to his question. The silence was broken when he said, *"Well?"*

"Well what?" I said in frustration.

"Why didn't you just say you were visiting a relative?" he asked.

"Because I am not going to lie," I responded. *"Look,"* I continued, *"if you want someone to lie, then send somebody else. You can be mad at me if you want, but you should consider this first. If I won't lie for you, you can have confidence that I won't lie to you either."*

And with that, he ended the conversation by saying, *"I'll see you on Monday morning."* He hung up without saying goodbye.

To be perfectly honest with you, I didn't know if I was going to have a job on Monday morning when I came into the office. I knew what I did was right, but I may be blamed for losing a valuable customer. The morning went on as normal, but just before lunch I heard the page come across the loud speakers, "Phil McKinney, please come to _____ office."

It wasn't abnormal to be paged to his office regularly, but this time my imagination was running wild. I didn't know what was going to happen.

When I entered his office, I scoped out all the available chairs for Human Resources' personnel. I had been a part of several dismissals of employees and knew the protocol.

To my delight and surprise, it was just him in the room. His countenance was good, and the atmosphere in the room felt good.

"Shut the door. Have a seat," he said as I entered. He jumped right in by saying, *"Good news. We have enough approved inventory to satisfy the order and have made arrangements to expedite the product to the customer."*

My sigh of relief was visible enough that he nodded his head as if to say, *"I feel the same way."*

He continued, *"I still need you to go to Toronto and fix that machine."*

My facial expression shifted, as did my posture. He raised his hand to stop me from speaking and said, *"We'll do it right."*

A Shift

There was a shift in our relationship from that day on — both professional and personal. The shift from *"boss"* to *"mentor"* began. It was noticeable enough that other managers and department heads were envious of what they perceived as favoritism. He trusted me with company information that was highly confidential as well as personal information.

On many occasions, he would walk down the hall to my office, close the door, and share his burdens. I sensed that I made the short list of people he could trust.

One morning before anyone arrived, I made my way down the hall to his office. I had waited for just the right time. It needed to be as normal of a day as possible. Without asking permission, I just entered his office and took a seat. *"I have something that I need to tell you."*

His eyes opened wide as he asked, *"You're not quitting, are you?"*

I smiled and said, *"No, nothing like that. I came in to say 'thank you' for being such a great mentor. I have learned so much from your leadership. I needed to tell you this during a time that it was clear that there were no strings attached – like review time."*

After he was convinced that I didn't have a hidden motive, he leaned back in his chair and said, *"You've made it easy. You have been a good student."*

Faithful in Little

I no longer work for the company. He is now retired, but we remain friends to this day. From time to time, I look back on that evening when I was rejected at the border. To think, I could have traded my credibility, influence, mentorship, and a lifelong friendship for a senseless compromise.

My character has been tested since then, and I believe it was the strength gained and lessons learned, like my interaction at the border, that prepared me for much more difficult temptations.

CHAPTER 11

P.E.A.K.

NO • EGO

P.E.A.K: Practical, Energized, Adjustable, Knowledgeable.

Learn

"Leaders are learners. When you stop learning, you stop leading." – Andy Stanley

Leaders Are Readers

Perhaps Harry Truman said it best, *"Not all readers are leaders, but all leaders are readers."*

I have greatly benefited from authors who share their knowledge and experiences. In some cases, it took them decades or even their lifetimes to learn what I can read about in less than a week's time.

It hardly seems fair, yet many choose not to take advantage of these resources. I recently came across a statistic that may encourage you to begin reading more. The average CEO reads thirty books a year, and the average person only reads one book per year. The average CEO makes 384 percent more money per year than the average person.

Coincidence? Maybe, but I doubt it.

There are many reasons why people don't take to reading. Some of which are legitimate challenges like dyslexia or comprehension challenges. I mean no insult to the individuals who have these challenges, but I also don't give a pass. Nearly every book these days is offered in an audio version. Something that I take advantage of while I drive. My car becomes a classroom. The average American spends more than 290 hours each year in a vehicle. That means you could listen to as many as fifteen books each year while you drive.

I will be honest, I didn't read more than a handful of books (like five) before I turned thirty years old. The problem for me was that I didn't find value in books because I was attempting to read the wrong style. I do not find enjoyment in reading fiction books like *Harry Potter*, *Hunger Games*, or love stories. I am not knocking those books or others like them. My wife loves reading those types of books. For her, it is like watching a television show or movie. I took a crack at a few non-fiction books, but they were basically regurgitation of what my social circle was already talking about. When someone in our association wrote a book, it seemed like it was simply more of the same. I made an unfair assumption that all books were going to be like that, so I didn't read.

I don't want to limit personal development and growth to reading alone. That wouldn't be accurate or even reasonable. Some people thrive in a classroom setting, at a conference, or while listening to a dynamic speaker. I have a passion to help people grow, so I began to build a library that consists of books, CDs, DVDs, and documentaries to lend. I have learned to ask people what their best or favorite style of learning is before offering one of my resources.

Whatever yours is, make a commitment to be a work in progress. I personally recommend a mix of every kind of learning style. Variety is the spice of life.

Who Is This Loud Mouth?

Part of new growth is making a commitment to exploration. The unknown is scary and some of the challenges that we face will appear to be unsurmountable.

It's in these moments that we need to encourage ourselves with past victories. One of the best examples of this is found in the Old Testament account of David facing a giant.

Unfortunately, this historical moment is often reduced to a children's story, and as such the impact is minimized. David is the youngest of his brothers and is tasked with the assignment to bring his brothers some meat and cheese. His brothers are in battle with the Philistine army and are in a showdown between one taunting warrior and the whole army.

When David arrives, he is appalled that nobody has stood up to this loud mouth instigator. David beseeches the King to be commissioned to oppose and kill this taunting warrior.

Not My First Rodeo

David's brothers were furious and accused him of being prideful. The King was impressed by David's willingness but initially rejected his proposal. After all, this was a hardened, war-tested, mammoth man, and David was young and inexperienced.

Or was he? David would not be turned away and pleaded his case to the King. David had been responsible for watching over his father's sheep and had stood between a lion and his father's herd. On another occasion he had stood toe to toe with a bear who had come to attack the sheep.

David told the King, *"The Lord delivered the lion and the bear unto my hands, and he will deliver this giant as well!"* 1 Samuel 17:37 (paraphrase). Boom!

Reminisce, Not Re-Live.

When facing the largest and most dangerous challenge of his life, David encouraged himself by remembering his past victories or accomplishments. We all need some lion and bear experiences and would do good to follow David's example and use them to encourage us when facing difficult challenges.

There is, however, a big difference between reminiscing about the past and living in the past. You know the type. It's the forty-eight-year-old, out of shape guy who still wears his letterman jacket from high school. He always likens whatever you're talking about to the *"big game"* of '89.

The same thing happens with leaders who stop learning and growing. They stop living in the present and attempt to relive the glory days. They are splashing around in yesterday's mud puddles instead of dancing in today's rain.

The trouble with yesterday's mud puddles is that they eventually dry up, and so do we. We need to stay fresh and current if we want to operate at our peak performance. You've worked too hard to accomplish what you have.

Your dream is not a destination; it is a journey. And a sure way to take your foot off the accelerator is to believe that you have "arrived." As a tool to ensure that I keep running at my peak performance, I have created an acronym out of the word P.E.A.K.

Practical

People are drawn to solutions and repulsed by problems. As a leader, you are a problem solver. A solution finder. A way maker. Your theories are great, but people are looking for methods that are effective in real life circumstances. As Albert Einstein said, *"If you can't explain it simply, you don't understand it well enough."*

Insecure leaders are more concerned about their egos than they are about helping people. More concerned about being perceived as smart than being helpful. This is a sure way to turn people off and lose your influence. If you lose your influence, then you're no longer leading. Allow me to pick on my profession for a minute.

As a pastor, my influence is largely based on people's willingness to attend a weekend gathering at the church that I lead. No one is forced or required. If I do a poor job at attracting, maintaining, and offering practical solutions to our community, my influence will be short lived. A good leader can process challenging concepts and principles and deliver them in a way that applies to everyday applications.

Religion has historically done a poor job at providing practical solutions to societal issues. Before the invention of the printing press, the priest and the church were the only ones with copies of the ancient scriptures. This led to many abuses and atrocities that have stained the history of the church. As John Dalberg-Acton says, *"Power tends to corrupt, and absolute power corrupts absolutely."*

In addition to the church having control of the ancient text, the presentation of the scripture was performed in Latin, a foreign language to most of the listening audience. This made church attendance a spectator sport instead of a classroom.

The church has come a long way, but she still struggles with relevance. I speak with many leaders, ministers, and pastors who struggle to discern the difference between *"methodology"* and *"theology."*

Methods are simply the delivery system, not the message itself. There was a period of time when people listened to vinyl records. It was cutting edge and modern. Soon the records shrank, and people listened to 45s. Then the invention of the 8-track tape revolutionized the way we listened to music. It made music mobile. Automobile manufacturers began to offer 8-track players as an option in their new vehicles. The 8-track led to the cassette tape and then CDs.

When my wife and I picked out our new Chevy Silverado truck in 2017, we were informed that it was the last year that General Motors was going to offer a CD player. Now we listen to music digitally or stream it through the onboard Wi-Fi. The delivery systems evolved with available technology.

You can be stubborn and hold on to your suitcase-sized container of 8-tracks, but you're not going to be able to connect them with today's vehicles.

The same is true for you and me. Our 20th Century methods are not going to connect with the 21st Century world. Methods are many, principles are few. Methods often change, but principles never do.

In order to remain relevant, it will require us to release old methods and be open to new ones. Imagine holding something so tightly in your hand that your knuckles are bright white. When your hand is clinched tight, it is not capable of receiving anything new. But if you release what you're holding, your hand is open and able to receive again.

This can be difficult because sometimes it requires letting go of things that we prefer. The question that must be addressed is whether you desire your preference over influence. Ditch your ego and lead.

2) Energized

There is a reason why professional sports teams have cheerleaders, mascots, and giant LED screens. To energize the crowd! Energy from the fans can be felt by the players on the field or on the court. It radiates. When teams are energized, they feel like they can achieve almost anything.

As a leader, everything you do is contagious. One of the most important characteristics of a leader is the ability to have a positive outlook and belief in what can be achieved. It is the confidence of a passionate leader that persuades a team to believe a task is possible. Emotion has a lot to do with accomplishment. Emotion is energy in motion. The direction of the motion, good or bad, will be determined by the energy of the leader.

An energized leader is magnetic and draws people in. When the leader is optimistic, happy, excited, and ready to storm hell with a water pistol, it makes people want to do the same thing. It is impressive how persuasive this is. Just watch an infomercial. You want to buy whatever they are peddling because they look so stinking happy!

One night I couldn't sleep, so I started flipping through the channels. I don't know how it is that I landed on the Food Network because I'm not really a big fan of cooking. I am, however, a big fan of eating, so something must have caught my attention. After forty-five minutes of watching this enthusiastic chef prepare meal after meal, I was ready to go to culinary school. I was sucked in like a fly to a zapper. It's the power of an energized person.

My friend Mike is a prime example of how someone's energy can assist you in going way beyond your perceived capabilities. I had been consistently jogging three miles on the treadmill all winter. I was jogging three to five times each week and feeling pretty good about it.

The winters in Wisconsin, where I was living at the time, seemed to last an eternity. The Spring weather was providing windows of opportunity to jog outside if someone was so inclined to do so. My friend Mike invited me to join him for a jog the following Saturday morning. He said, *"We can take off from my house and round the country block. It's just over five miles."*

My initial thought was, *"That's further than I have been going, but what's an extra two miles?"*

And so, I agreed to meet him.

Saturday morning rolled around, and it was a perfect Spring day. I was pumped! I was delighted that Mike was jogging at a moderate pace and not trying to treat our jog like a race. Mile one was a breeze, and so was mile two.

When we hit the three-mile mark, it was as if someone pulled the batteries out of me. My legs, lungs, and mind were conditioned for three miles, and I was in trouble. I was able to press through and keep my discomfort quiet from Mike for another half mile. In between gasps for air, I was able to sputter out, *"Mike ... you're going to ... have to go on ahead of me ... I am spent."*

Mike looked at me as if I were speaking another language. Then he said, *"No way, Philly* (his nickname for me). *You've got this! Just slow your pace, and we'll get through it together."*

And so, I did, even though everything in me wanted to lay down on the side of the road.

My pace was so slow that I was moving forward slower than I would normally walk. I was spent! Mike wanted to keep his pace, so he literally jogged in circles around me as I made my way down the country road. All the while chanting, shouting, and encouraging me. A few times he ducked into fields to give me an opportunity to get ahead, and then he would return to the road and catch up with me.

He did this the entire time until we returned to his driveway. It was Mike's energy that got me through the final two miles of that jog. His motivation made me feel that if I quit, I wasn't quitting on me, I was quitting on him. It's the power of an energized leader.

When we walk into a dark room, it is our first instinct to reach for a light switch. Why? To see where we are going, find what we're looking for, or complete a task. Great leaders are like a light switch. A light switch completes a circuit, and a positively charged neutron energizes another, starting a chain reaction. The chain reaction continues until the light illuminates. The light switch wasn't the source of the electricity, but it was responsible for making the connection needed to accomplish the task. And so it is with an energized leader.

3/ Adjustable

When I was nineteen years old, I attended my first ministry training program. I can still hear Dr. Barclay's voice in my head saying, *"Blessed are the flexible, for they shall not be broken!"*

I have had to speak these words to myself dozens of times throughout my professional and ministerial life. Rigidity will cause you to break under pressure, and as a leader, people are especially looking to you in times of pressure.

Flexible leaders are those who can modify their style or approach to leadership in response to uncertain or unpredictable circumstances. Leadership is not "one size fits all." In today's fast-paced, rapidly changing, globally diverse business environment, flexibility is an absolute necessity. Leaders must be able to respond quickly in an increasingly complex work environment. However, simply being open to ideas is not enough to make an effective flexible leader.

Leaders need to identify circumstances in which their old techniques are not working. From there, they need to decide how to approach the problem, including what new behaviors or methods are viable and which will accomplish their goals. And most importantly, act. Leaders aren't the only individuals who need to be flexible for an organization to be successful.

Encouraging team members to be more flexible in their own work will aid in developing their flexibility skills. Followers who are more flexible understand the need for changing behaviors with changing circumstances. If your team understands the value of flexibility, they will be more open to any changes suggested by their leaders.

Tomorrow's leaders must learn to treat uncertainty as the new normal. Being flexible includes large changes, but also trickles down to everyday activities that are subject to change.

Knowledge

To grow, gaining as much knowledge as possible is important. Knowledge is more than science, technology, and the fields we study in books.

Knowledge is also very important to shape our personality and perfect our behavior and dealings with people. Knowledge is the key to relevance, vibrance, and peak performance. Perhaps Harvey Ullman says it best, *"Anyone who stops learning is old, whether this happens at twenty or eighty. Anyone who keeps on learning not only remains young but becomes constantly more valuable regardless of physical capacity."*

The curious leader is the one who ignites the genius within his team. He invites others to ask *"Why?"* and challenges the status quo. Knowledge is a combination of creativity and criticism. Criticism doesn't have to be mean-spirited or be directed at an individual. Criticism can be an intolerance of an unreasonable procedure, policy, or method. It is amazing how customs and traditions that have very little common sense can be passed down for generations.

Once challenged, it usually becomes apparent to everyone else. But someone needs to ask, *"Why?"* Let's look at the following example:

> *A husband and his wife were in their kitchen. The husband was sitting at the kitchen table reading the newspaper while his wife was preparing a ham for dinner. The husband watched the wife cut off about one inch from either end of the ham. He asked why she cut the end off, proclaiming, "That's a waste of good ham!"*
>
> *She said, "That's the way my mom prepared the ham."*
>
> *The husband asked, "Why did your mom cut the ends off?"*

The wife didn't know.

Later, the wife called her mom to find out why she cut the ends of the ham off. Her mom said, "Because that was the way my mom prepared ham."

The wife's grandma had passed away several years earlier, but her Grandpa was still living. She called her Grandpa and asked, "Grandpa, why did Grandma cut the ends off of the ham?"

He was silent as he thought for a moment. Then he replied, "So the ham could fit in the baking pan."

Gaining new information and deeper understanding has a direct effect on how we feel about ourselves. It is difficult, if not impossible, to operate in confidence when you feel ill-informed or ill-prepared. Brilliant teachers and instructors are not the ones who tell us *what* to learn, but rather *how* to learn.

I was fortunate to work in several manufacturing settings and environments. The range was vast and included locations that were certified clean rooms and environmentally controlled to machining centers and stamping presses.

What I discovered was that there are two types of Industrial Maintenance Mechanics. There are those who are experts in their facility and environment by sheer memorization and familiarity of the equipment. But if you remove them from their familiar equipment, they are lost.

The other type of mechanic is the one who can apply universal troubleshooting principles in any industrial setting. They confidently approach each new piece of equipment as an exciting new challenge. Confidence leads to hope. I recently heard someone say, "The person who possesses the most hope will have the greatest influence."

A hope-filled leader becomes an architect of a hope-filled culture. Hope is "an expectation of good." When we approach a challenge with an expectation that a path will be found, the mind begins to search for a way.

My biggest encouragement is to remain humble, teachable, hungry, and curious.

For us to operate at P.E.A.K performance, we must commit to being lifelong learners. As William Pollard says, "Learning and innovation go hand in hand. The arrogance of success is to think that what you did yesterday will be sufficient for tomorrow."

CHAPTER 12

It Isn't for the Faint of Heart

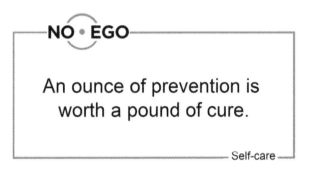

*"An empty lantern provides no light. Self-care is the
fuel that allows your light to shine brightly."*
— Unknown

Peace of Mind

Leadership requires constant maintenance and
attention. Wouldn't it be great if vision could be cast
once, team building could happen once a year, and
everyone on the team would just buy in?

If you're like me, you have a hard time leading
yourself, let alone being a catalyst for others to grow,
get plugged in, and develop. There is a real
temptation to overly focus on the business, ministry, or
team and neglect the condition of your own soul. We

think we're being noble by putting others first, but the day will come when you attempt to pour into somebody and there is nothing to give.

Nearly every leader that I have met struggles or has struggled with weariness, and many of them didn't address it until tragedy struck. Hard. Some of them have suffered heart attacks, strokes, or crippling anxiety attacks. The stress and the pressure build, and like a soda pop that has been shaken, it erupts uncontrollably. And when it does, it will happen at the most inconspicuous time and will be as shocking to you as the people that catch the brunt of the explosion.

The English translators of the Bible use four words to describe our minds. This has caused confusion for some when they read certain scriptures. The words soul, heart, life, and mind are all used to describe the seat of emotions, will, and intellect. The Bible is a collection of books from various authors over thousands of years. The importance of the mind is captured by these books and written in different eras.

There have been hundreds if not thousands of books written on the subject, emphasizing the importance and power of our minds. And for good reason. Our minds are like Velcro.

It's Not Working Anymore

Have you noticed that over time Velcro picks up lint and debris? After a while, it becomes so full of foreign objects that it loses its stickiness and hinders its very purpose.

The same is true with our minds. If we don't learn the art of cleansing our minds, we will eventually become so full of foreign debris that it will hinder our purpose. The point of discovery usually happens when you attempt to do one more "*normal*" task, and you've got nothing! And you wonder if you will ever have it again. Some never do, but that doesn't have to be you.

The key is not being a great starter; the key is being a great finisher. The secret sauce to finishing well is becoming a guardian of your mind. No one will do this for you, and if you don't, you will diminish your potential.

King Solomon wrote that the single most important thing we can do is guard our minds. Proverbs 4:23 (TPT) says,

> "So above all, guard the affections of your heart, for they affect all that you are. Pay attention to the welfare of your innermost being, for from there flows the wellspring of life."

What You Think About, You Bring About

As Abraham Lincoln said, "*The best way to predict your future is to create it.*"

Studies reveal that the average person has sixty to eighty thousand thoughts per day. The unfortunate reality is that as high as ninety percent of them are the same thoughts each day. The meditation of thought has a profound influence on us and will impact our personality.

When you allow an emotional state to remain for hours or days, it's called a mood. If you allow that same emotional reaction to continue for weeks or months, it becomes a temperament. Temperament, if continued for months or years, becomes a personality trait.

Generally speaking, our brains are a record of the past. Rehearsing those same thoughts and imaginations bring about the same results. When we change our thoughts, we begin to fire and create new neuropaths in the brain. When we meditate, focus, and think on new things, we are essentially putting ourselves in a state of creation. In his book, *You Are the Placebo*, Dr. Joe Dispenza writes, "The brain then is not just a record of the past, it becomes a map unto the future."

All Plugged Up

This takes real intentionality and focused energy. Our brains will begin to pick up debris from our environment much like the furnace filter at your house. Have you forgotten to check your filter for an extended period? I have, and it is shocking how dark and polluted it becomes. The filter's primary function is to dictate what particles can flow into your home.

In time, it gets saturated with debris. When this happens, it not only begins to restrict the flow of warm or cool air, but it also begins to pass pollutants into the house.

I believe this illustrates what King Solomon is saying in Proverbs chapter 4 about our hearts (minds). When we don't pay attention to our "innermost being," it is like ignoring the filter in your furnace. The flow of life from within us will be hindered. In time, this will begin to pollute our lives. It will show up in the words we use, our response to challenges, our temperament, and our energy. When the thought alone of facing the day is overwhelming, it may be a sign that your filter is dirty.

A Little Goes a Long Way

Benjamin Franklin famously advised fire-threatened Philadelphians in 1736 that *"an ounce of prevention is worth a pound of cure."*

Part of guarding our hearts is learning to manage our minds like a gardener manages his garden. If the gardener neglects the garden, the weeds take over. It becomes overwhelming.

Soon enough, it is difficult to recognize what belongs and what does not. Weeds don't just add up, they multiply. Preventive maintenance is never convenient and is easy to put off until another time. Putting it off exaggerates the problem.

In the early 1970s, Fram Oil Filters ran a series of commercials featuring an auto mechanic urging people to change their oil and oil filter routinely (of course using a Fram oil filter). To make his point to the consumers, he coined the famous slogan, *"You can pay me now, or you can pay me later."*

In other words, you can pay a little for an oil change and new filter now or a lot for an engine rebuild later. The same is true for our mental longevity and success.

Stressed Out

Scientists have been able to identify a stress hormone that is released from the brain when it perceives an imminent danger. Stress is a gift that is intended to elevate our senses in order to survive. Once the threat has passed, the chemistry in the body returns to normal.

But what if it doesn't? Humans are the only known creatures who can release the stress hormone without an actual life-threatening event. We can release the hormone by thought alone. Our bodies are not designed to operate under prolonged stress. People who live in a perpetual state of stress are much more susceptible to illness and chronic conditions like high blood pressure, anxiety, and digestive disturbances.

Simply put, we can think ourselves sick. On the bright side, we can also think ourselves well. This isn't a new discovery.

Nearly three thousand years ago, King Solomon wrote what science is now confirming on this topic. Proverbs 17:22 (NKJV) says,

> "A merry heart does good, like medicine, but a broken spirit dries the bones."

Remember, the English translators often used the word "heart" in place of the word "mind." A cheerful mind is like medicine to our bodies? That right!

Dr. Sven Svenbak of the Norwegian University of Science and Technology tracked fifty-four thousand Norwegians for seven years and discovered that individuals who found life the funniest lived longer. In fact, people were thirty-five percent more likely to survive longer.

In 2015, the journal Psychosomatic Medicine published "A 15-Year Follow Up Study of Sense of Humor and Causes of Mortality." The study followed over fifty-three thousand participants and found a sense of humor was positively associated with survival for people with cardiovascular disease and infections. A sense of humor provides a very real health-protecting and coping mechanism that ultimately leads to longer life.

Other studies show that hearty laughter, just like exercise, decreases arterial stiffness, contributes to better blood sugar regulation in diabetics, and can improve cancer-killing cells.

Not surprisingly, laughter can also decrease stress, increase pain tolerance, reduce depression, and improve overall quality of life.

It's Not All Laughs

But let's be honest, life isn't always humorous. Pastor Judah Smith says, *"Life has a way of touching us all."* And he knows firsthand. Judah Smith is the lead pastor of one of the largest and fastest growing churches in Washington State, and he now has an additional campus in Los Angeles. Pastor Judah's reach and influence is massive. He has more than two hundred thousand Twitter followers, multiple best-selling books, and frequently sold out auditoriums for his speeches.

In 2009, Judah's dad (and hero) passed away after fighting cancer. Wendel was the dynamic founding pastor of The City Church. It was a crushing loss to the community, and especially to Judah. A legacy could have been lost had Judah not been raised to understand the heart of gratitude. Something that his pastor/dad had demonstrated.

When asked about the influence his dad had on him, Judah said, "*Watching my dad preach was pretty special. I always wanted to be like my dad – he was probably a better man outside the pulpit than he was in – and he was a great preacher.*"

Gratitude is powerful. Gratitude puts you in a mental posture of receiving. Most generally, we are grateful because we have received something like a gift or a compliment. A heart of gratitude is a proactive approach to looking for a positive outcome.

Metaphorically speaking, it is lifting our focus from the situation to the Source. The palmist writes in Psalms 3:3 (NIV),

 "*But you, LORD, are a shield around me, my glory, the One who lifts my head high.*"

What Are You Looking At?

My friend Dr. Keith Johnson eloquently puts it this way, "*Where attention goes, energy flows, and results show.*"

A grateful heart will redirect our attention from the circumstance to the One who heals, delivers, and sets free – Jesus. It is easy to celebrate, praise, and glorify God when things are going great. And we should.

But God's goodness doesn't change when we are going through difficulty. I have discovered that worship is most powerful when I don't "feel" like it, and the act of worship changes me and my environment.

The Apostle Paul and his travel companion, Silas, were on one of their routine missionary trips. They were spreading a message of hope, salvation, freedom, and a whole new way of being human. A message that transforms people and destroys the power of darkness and religion.

They encountered a slave girl who was demon possessed and delivered her from the influence of darkness. Great for her, but bad for her owner. The young girl's owner made money from her demon-empowered ability, and he was furious to have lost his income. He brought Paul and Silas before the Macedonian magistrates and had them charged with a crime.

As a result, they were whipped, beaten with rods, and placed in prison. The inner-prison. The men were standing in human waste, chained to the filthy prison wall, with open bloody wounds. I'm not sure that it gets much worse than that.

Talk about an opportunity to complain. What did they do? They worshipped. Luke, the writer of the book of Acts, records in Acts 16:25-26 (NKJV),

> "But at midnight Paul and Silas were praying and singing hymns to God, and the prisoners were listening to them. Suddenly there was a great earthquake, so that the foundations of the prison were shaken; and immediately all the doors were opened, and everyone's chains were loosed."

It's Bad But He's Good

These two men demonstrated the power of worship, gratitude, and thanksgiving in all circumstances. They determined within themselves that they worship not because their circumstances are good, but because God is good.

And look what happened. Chains broke, prison doors opened, and people suffering the same pain watched a miracle happen. There is no way to avoid every external circumstance, but there is a way to protect ourselves from allowing the outside pressure to crush us. It's by being filled with gratitude.

Under Pressure

Have you ever polished off a bottle of water and crushed the plastic bottle before throwing it away or recycling it? Sure, you have. It was almost effortless to crush the empty bottle.

Take that same plastic bottle filled with water and attempt to crush it. You'll never do it. The same is true for you and me. The pressure may be great, but we will not be crushed if we remain full of gratitude. This is vitally important to take seriously and be intentional about. You must first care for yourself before you can serve others.

I fly routinely, and I can almost give the flight attendant safety speech from memory. Remember this portion:

> *"In the unlikely event of a loss of cabin pressure, panels above your seat will open revealing oxygen masks. Reach up and pull a mask toward you. Place it over your nose and mouth, and secure with the elastic band that can be adjusted to ensure a snug fit. The plastic bag will not fully inflate, although oxygen is flowing.* **Secure your own mask first before helping others.**"

Notice that curious last sentence. Why should you secure your own mask first before helping others? Isn't that selfish? What if your small child is seated next to you and is gasping for air? What if your elderly mother is traveling with you and needs help? Are you really supposed to look out for Number One? Yes.

Of what use will you be to your child or mother if you have lost consciousness because of a lack of oxygen? In this emergency, we can see the importance of taking care of ourselves. For some reason, though, when we start to think about all our different responsibilities, many of us feel guilty taking care of our physical, mental, and spiritual health. But you cannot give what you do not possess.

For approximately thirteen years, the Apostle Paul traveled tens of thousands of miles on missionary journeys and visited most of the known world. His letters make up nearly two-thirds of the New Testament and are filled with instruction and encouragement.

What many don't realize is that a great deal of his writing was done from prison cells. He spent five of his thirteen years of ministry in prison. And the prison system of his day would make our modern-day incarceration environments look like penthouses in comparison. If there were a person who had reason to complain, it was Paul. The Apostle Paul was not just a dissimilator of his message, he was a practitioner. He knew firsthand the power of staying full of gratitude.

How did he do it? While in custody, he wrote to the church in Philippi to follow his example.

Philippians 4:4-9 (TPT) says,

> "Be cheerful with joyous celebration in every season of life. Let joy overflow, for you are united with the Anointed One! Let gentleness be seen in every relationship, for our Lord is ever near. Don't be pulled in different directions or worried about a thing. Be saturated in prayer throughout each day, offering your faith-filled requests before God with overflowing gratitude. Tell him every detail of your life, then God's wonderful peace that transcends human understanding, will make the answers known to you through Jesus Christ. So keep your thoughts continually fixed on all that is authentic and real, honorable and admirable, beautiful and respectful, pure and holy, merciful and kind. And fasten your thoughts on every glorious work of God, praising him always. Follow the example of all that we have imparted to you and the God of peace will be with you in all things."

Peace Is Priceless

It requires participation on our end, but if we follow Paul's example, we are assured that "peace will be with us in all things."

I have not mastered this, but I can testify that when I am saturated in prayer, overflowing with gratitude, fixing my thoughts continually on what is good, I experience peace when everything around me tells me that I should not. I have come to value peace more than ever before. I pay attention when I don't have peace, and I find out quickly what has disrupted it.

For me, peace is priceless, and I will guard it with my life. And so should you.

CEO

No one will do it for you. You are the CEO of your life. Hire, fire, and promote accordingly. You alone are the gatekeeper of your mind. You decide what you see, what and who you listen to, and what you allow to accumulate.

If you're feeling heavy and tired, learn to rest, not quit. You must make downtime a priority. No one will schedule it for you. The same people who demand all your time, expect you to be superhuman, and criticize you for not meeting their needs, will be the same ones who will criticize you when your marriage fails, your kids hate you, and you burn out.

Remind people that you set boundaries to respect yourself, not to offend them.

They're Counting on You

Part of being strong is asking for help. Ditch your ego and ask for help. As the old African proverb goes, "If you want to go fast, go alone. If you want to go far, go together."

Make a determined commitment to be a great finisher, not just a great starter. The world needs what you have. You are uniquely gifted to meet the need of something or someone.

Your gift is not for you, it is for serving others. You owe it to your generation to take care of yourself and to cultivate greatness from within you. You are worth the investment.

End Notes

Page 64, Christopher Pappas, January 29, 2016, "8 Important Characteristics of Baby Boomers eLearning Professionals should know."

Page 65, www.sage.com, "2015 State of The Start Up, Survey Report."

Page 67, www.apa.org, "Stress by Generation."

Page 67, www.time.com, 2015, "Americans Check Their Phones 8 Billion Times a Day."

Page 67, www.techcrunch.com, March 03, 2017, "U.S. Consumers Now Spend 5 Hours Per Day on Mobile Devices."

What Others Are Saying

I'm a firm believer that everyone has a story. Some people hide their story while others tell their story and empower others to succeed. That's exactly what Phil McKinney has done with *No Ego*. His honest, candid approach will no doubt challenge you to take a deeper look at your own ego and make the necessary adjustments in order to rise to the next level of your life. It's an easy and simple read, yet filled with powerful and practical information that anyone can apply to their life. It's a must read for anyone that is ready for more out of life.

— Adonis Lenzy
Author, Speaker, TV Show Host — Nashville, TN

This book is filled with great wisdom and insights. The kind received through hard earned experience. The humorous stories and great quotes help establish those truths he shared. I am already looking forward to Phil's next book.

— Pastor Lee Armstrong
Author, Associate Pastor — Durant, OK

www.noegocc.com